D0143804

Opening Dialogue

UNDERSTANDING THE DYNAMICS OF LANGUAGE AND LEARNING IN THE ENGLISH CLASSROOM

Martin Nystrand

WITH

Adam Gamoran, Robert Kachur, & Catherine Prendergast

FOREWORD BY ROBERT GUNDLACH

Teachers College, Columbia University
New York and London

Published by Teachers College Press, 1234 Amsterdam Avenue, New York, NY 10027

Library of Congress Cataloging-in-Publication Data

Nystrand, Martin.
    Opening dialogue : understanding the dynamics of language and learning in the English classroom / Martin Nystrand, with Adam Gamoran, Robert Kachur & Catherine Prendergast ; foreword by Robert Gundlach.
        p.   cm. — (Language and literacy series)
    Includes bibliographical references (p.   ) and index.
    ISBN 0-8077-3574-4 (cloth : alk. paper). — ISBN 0-8077-3573-6 (paper : alk. paper)
    1. Language arts (Secondary) — United States.   2. Literature — Study and teaching (Secondary) — United States.   3. Teacher-student relationships — United States.
    4. Interaction analysis in education — United States.   I. Title.   II. Series: Language and literacy series (New York, N.Y.)
    LB1631.N97   1997
    428'.0071'2 — dc20   96-32840

ISBN 0-8077-3573-6 (paper)
ISBN 0-8077-3574-4 (cloth)

Printed on acid-free paper
Manufactured in the United States of America

04 03 02 01 00 99 98 97   8 7 6 5 4 3 2 1

The will to learn is an intrinsic motive, one that finds both its source and its reward in its own exercise. The will to learn becomes a "problem" only under specialized circumstances like those of a school, where a curriculum is set, students confined, and a path fixed. The problem exists not so much in learning itself, but in the fact that what the school imposes often fails to enlist the natural energies that sustain spontaneous learning—curiosity, a desire for competence, aspiration to emulate a model, and a deep-sensed commitment to the web of social reciprocity.
                    —Jerome Bruner, *Toward a Theory of Instruction*

Contents

Foreword

OPENING DIALOGUE deserves the thoughtful consideration of the large audience of scholars and teachers that I expect it will reach. In fact, I would not be surprised if this volume eventually earned the status of a classic in its field, akin, perhaps, to Janet Emig's influential monograph, *The Composing Processes of Twelfth Graders* (1971). Although the two research projects, separated as they are by a quarter-century of dramatic shifts of emphasis in the study of language, differ conspicuously in subject, scope, and method, the two volumes resemble each other in interesting ways. Both present innovative studies imaginatively conceived and carefully executed. And both articulate fresh perspectives on fundamental issues in the learning and teaching of English. With *The Composing Processes of Twelfth Graders,* Janet Emig reoriented our thinking about how older adolescents, working largely on their own, compose pieces of writing. With OPENING DIALOGUE, Martin Nystrand and his colleagues promise to reorient our thinking about how younger adolescents and their teachers, talking together, compose shared understandings that in turn contribute to individual students' learning.

As he presents the conceptual framework for the studies reported in this volume, Nystrand argues that people learn not merely by being spoken (or written) to, but by participating in communicative exchanges. Learning emerges from the interplay of voices. Thus a dialogic analysis of learning, Nystrand says, seeks to understand students' learning from the angle of studying students' "responses to the voices of teachers, texts, and peers." The focal point of this research is neither the teacher alone nor the student alone; nor is it the jointly constructed "text" (if one imagines a transcript as a text) created over time by all of the participants in a discussion. Rather, the spotlight is on particular exchanges between participants. Nystrand is interested, first, in what each participant learns from the particular interactions that constitute the conversational steps or moves in a classroom discussion. He then considers alternative patterns of interaction and asks which pattern seems to contribute most effectively to students' learning.

By formulating these ideas into a framework for empirical inquiry, Nystrand brings into the tradition of research on classroom talk a set of powerful arguments from Bakhtin and especially from Rommetveit—"the developing human mind," Rommetveit (1992) recently asserted, "is dialogically constituted" (p. 23). Nystrand's formulations also resonate with ideas expressed by contemporary philosophers—Charles Taylor (1994), for example, has argued that "the genesis of the human mind is . . . not monological, not something each person accomplishes on his or her own, but dialogical" (p. 32)—and by developmental psychologists interested in the human capacity for establishing joint attention with others. "I find it ironic," Jerome Bruner (1995) recently observed, "that in all the lists of human instincts that used to be offered by psychologists to explain human nature, nobody ever mentioned 'the need to share the objects of our attention with others'" (p. 12).

Nystrand's own previous theoretical work contributes two important ideas to the empirical framework he offers here. First, in his earlier studies of the structure of written communication (Nystrand, 1986), he succeeded in extending principles used in the analysis of spoken dialogue to the task of analyzing the communicative exchange implied in the use of written language. Given this advance, it thus becomes possible in the studies reported here to consider the interaction not only between a speaker and a listener but also between a writer and a reader, even when writer and reader meet only on the page. Second, Nystrand's earlier comparative theoretical work (1992) provides the basis for his emphasis in this volume on the distinction between theories of the social construction of meaning and theories of social interaction. Theories of the social construction of meaning concentrate on the relatively stable, widely shared understandings that groups of people develop for themselves. Theories of social interaction, in contrast, highlight the more dynamic, less predictable meanings created when two or more people engage in conversation. In the studies reported in this volume, Nystrand and his colleagues concentrate on social interaction—that is, on how meanings emerge and change as people ask and answer questions. This emphasis allows Nystrand and his colleagues to study specific traces of students' learning-in-progress as these traces are evident in transcripts of classroom talk. By directing our attention to the continual unfolding of meaning in social interaction, Nystrand and his colleagues remind us that, given the freedom and uncertainties of genuine conversation, learning is often built on surprises.

If the perspective Martin Nystrand offers is promising, both in its account of how people learn and in its implications for how teachers can organize classroom discussion to promote learning, the news from the main empirical study Nystrand and Adam Gamoran report is not encouraging. To judge from the many hours of classroom discussion Nystrand and Gamoran have analyzed, teachers leading classroom discussions mostly talk while students listen—if indeed they listen. Against this backdrop of a preponderance of monologue, however, a number of instances of genuine dialogue stand out. Nystrand and his colleagues examine these cases to consider how they work and how they seem to affect students' learning. The investigators find that, compared with discussions characterized by a patchwork of monologic utterances, dialogically organized instruction establishes higher expectations for students' learning, engages students more fully with the material of the curriculum, and coaches students in the use of more complex patterns of thought. A closer look at two specific classroom discussion sessions confirms that teachers play a key role in shaping the kind of talk — and presumably therefore the kind of learning — their students experience.

The concluding chapter in this volume offers guidance for teachers, derived both from this research and from other recent studies. Throughout the interesting and potentially very useful advice presented in this chapter, a reader listening carefully can hear echoes of, or perhaps responses to, the voices of some of Martin Nystrand's own mentors. There is, for example, more than a trace of the voice of James Britton, who understood with remarkable insight the powerful role listening can play in effective teaching. And there is the voice of Wallace Douglas, who liked to correct teachers who complained that students "have nothing to say" — add "to me," Douglas would insist.

As I have suggested, I expect that Martin Nystrand and his colleagues may change the way we think about how the structure of classroom discussion affects students' learning. The advance in understanding they offer here, the progress in the continuing dialogue about this subject that their work constitutes, promises fresh ways to consider still broader issues. With a clearer picture of how the structure of discussion can promote high expectations for learning, strengthen students' engagement with material, and demonstrate complex patterns of reasoning, we will, for example, be in a better position to ask new questions about how students learn the content of any given curriculum. It is important to note that a dialogic approach to instruction, as Nystrand defines it, does not preclude placing value on engaging students in the study of rich and demanding material. In fact, an emphasis on dialogue suggests a process of learning analogous to the process of archaeology — the process, that is, of making and remaking understandings of what others knew, thought, felt, or did, perhaps elsewhere, perhaps long ago.

Of course, the making of such understandings begins very early in life, and it is a process of making sense of others but also a process of shaping a sense of ourselves. Interacting with other voices is at its core. Research of the kind Nystrand and his colleagues present offers us this lesson. So do other writers, working in different forms. In his Nobel Lecture, "Crediting Poetry," the poet Seamus Heaney (1995) describes his experience as a child in wartime, listening at night to the voices of his parents in the next room. Mingled with the intonations of these familiar voices was the steady radio voice of the BBC news reader, whose solemn monologue was in turn pocked by "the frantic, piercing signaling of Morse code" (p. 27). "Without needing to be theoretically instructed," Heaney observes, "consciousness quickly realizes that it is the site of variously contending discourses" (p. 28). In just this way, he suggests, the "child in the bedroom" was "already being schooled for the complexities of his adult predicament, a future where he would have to adjudicate among promptings" (p. 28). Heaney's reflections suggest, it seems to me, what Martin Nystrand and his colleagues help to illuminate in this volume: how conversation not only contributes new voices to an individual's consciousness, but also how participating in conversations, perhaps especially participating in conversations designed deliberately as part of an education, helps each of us learn ways to adjudicate wisely among promptings through the course of a life.

Robert Gundlach
Northwestern University

REFERENCES

Bruner, J. (1995). From joint attention to the meeting of minds: An introduction. In C. Moore & P. J. Dunham (Eds.), *Joint attention: Its origin and role in development* (pp. 1–14). Hillsdale, NJ: Erlbaum.

Emig, J. (1971). *The composing processes of twelfth graders* (Research Rep. No. 13). Urbana, IL: National Council of Teachers of English.

Heaney, S. (1995, December 25). Crediting poetry: The Nobel lecture. *The New Republic,* pp. 27–34.

Nystrand, M. (1986). *The structure of written communication: Studies in reciprocity between writers and readers.* Orlando & London: Academic Press.

Nystrand, M. (1992). Social interactionism versus social constructionism: Bakhtin, Rommetveit, and the semiotics of written text. In A. H. Wold (Ed.), *The dialogical alternative: Towards a theory of language and mind* (pp. 157–173). Oslo: Scandinavian University Press.

Rommetveit, R. (1992). Outlines of a dialogically based cognitive-social approach to human cognition and communication. In A. H. Wold (Ed.), *The dialogical alternative: Towards a theory of language and mind* (pp. 19–44). Oslo: Scandinavian University Press.

Taylor, C. (1994). The politics of recognition. In A. Gutman (Ed.), *Multiculturalism* (pp. 25–73). Princeton, NJ: Princeton University Press.

Preface

The education reform movement recently has proposed and examined many ways of restructuring American schools, including alternative classroom arrangements such as collaborative learning and small groups, upgraded credential requirements and competency testing for teachers, new curricula, merit pay, and modifications in teacher training. One aspect of schooling that only now is being examined closely as a candidate for restructuring concerns the kinds of instructional interactions that improve student learning. Some of these studies have called attention to unconventional forms of instruction such as small-group work and collaborative learning involving students working together, sustained discussion or "instructional conversation," and reciprocal teaching, in which students take turns teaching each other reading. Studies that have focused particularly on the role of classroom discourse in learning have renewed criticism of recitation as the persistent, dominant mode of instruction. In research on writing instruction, researchers have looked closely at the potential of response groups and teacher–student conferences to understand how different types of interaction can affect writing development.

In English instruction, part of this interest can be traced to pedagogical reforms initiated by James Britton and Nancy Martin in language arts education in England during the 1960s. Britton and Martin argued that instruction in language arts should be defined not by teaching knowledge about language and composition so much as by situating all student learning in terms of language in use, including both writing and talk. Useful learning tasks not only help students learn to write; they also enable students to "write to learn" (Martin, D'Arcy, Newton, & Parker, 1976). In the United States, this idea of writing as a way of knowing — or better, *coming* to know — helped shape the writing-across-the-curriculum movement as we know it today. In addition to writing to learn, Britton also articulated a notion of "talking to learn" (Britton, 1969), which has been less influential in American curricular reform than writing to learn. Calling talk "the ocean on which all else floats," Britton argued that engaged discussion, substantive teacher–student interaction, and peer-group work should be essential parts of any classroom context. Together, Martin and Britton articulated a vision of learning intrinsically tied to the active language processes of the learners.

The most recent research picks up many of these themes, but it seeks to be more specific about the classroom environment and teacher–student and peer relationships as they affect learning. This new focus on teacher–student and peer interaction has coincided with new conceptions of language and learning, especially viewing language not as a vehicle for the one-way transmission of knowledge from teacher to student but rather as a dynamic social and epistemic process of constructing and negotiating knowledge. The work of Russians Lev Vygotsky and Mikhail Bakhtin on discourse as a dialogic, sociocultural process has been seminal in these new conceptions. Vygotsky's sociocultural studies, for example, explicate the central role played by social interaction in conditioning the development of thinking and writing. Bakhtin's dialogic studies illuminate the semiotic process whereby the meaning of any given instance of discourse is dynamically structured by the interaction of the conversants, including writers and readers.

Dialogic Instruction examines the role of classroom and other instructional discourse in learning in eighth- and ninth-grade literature classes. This study was conducted under the auspices of the federally funded National Center on Effective Secondary Schools at the University of Wisconsin. Confronted with widespread, recent critiques of instruction in American schools as orderly but lifeless, superficial, and unchallenging, my colleagues and I chose to focus on the character of classroom discourse, as well as writing and reading tasks, for their effects on literature achievement. Our project was conducted over 2 years in dozens of middle and high schools (both public and parochial) in several midwestern urban, suburban, and rural communities. In all, 112 eighth- and ninth-grade language arts and English classes participated in this largest-ever study of classroom discourse and its effects on learning; more than 1,100 students and their teachers participated each year. We observed and collected data in about 450 class sessions. A special focus concerned differentials in instruction among low-, regular-, and high-track classes.

Despite an emerging consensus about the sociocultural foundations and character of discourse, we discovered that most schooling continues to be based on a transmission and recitation model of communication. Teachers talk and students listen. Our project sought specifically to relate student learning about literature to the nature of classroom discourse and the character of teacher–student interaction. By examining and assessing these matters through a dialogic lens of sociocultural theory, the study attempted to discover, as Wertsch (1991) puts it, "how the forms of discourse encountered in . . . formal schooling provide the underlying framework within which concept development occurs" (p. 116).

Acknowledgments

THE RESEARCH REPORTED in this book was sponsored by the National Center on Effective Secondary Schools, which operated from December 1985 to February 1991, and was supported by a grant from the U. S. Department of Education, Office of Educational Research and Improvement (Grant No. G-008690007-89) and by the Wisconsin Center for Education Research, School of Education, University of Wisconsin–Madison. Any opinions, findings, and conclusions or recommendations expressed in this publication are those of the authors and do not necessarily reflect the views of the supporting agencies.

I am greatly indebted to my research collaborator and friend Adam Gamoran, a sociologist whose quantitative skills, extraordinary administrative abilities, and unfailing collegiality touched every aspect of this project. I am also indebted to the tireless research support provided by project assistants Mark Berends, Dae-dong Hahn, Mary Jo Heck, John Knapp, and Jim Ladwig, and also the contributions of the many teachers and students who participated in the study, especially Nancy Jesse and Nora Platt. Stephen Fox, Carol Franko, Elaine Klein, Susan Koenig, Mary Morzinski, Marcia Reddick, Mark Scarborough, and Lorna Wiedemann served as readers and evaluators of student tests. Mary Jo Heck, Joan Parks, and Marcia Reddick proofed and revised all classroom discourse data. Special thanks go to Mary Jo Heck for also listening to tapes of all ninth-grade classes and verifying computer transcripts of all class observations, as well as for managing the entire data set of classroom discourse. Craig Wienhold provided invaluable programming assistance for Class 2.0 and Class-Edit 2.0, programs we used to collect and analyze classroom discourse data.

I am grateful for insightful comments on this research by Courtney Cazden and Elizabeth Cohen, who served as advisers to the project. Many others provided comments and useful feedback: Arthur Applebee and Judith Langer and various faculty and students associated with the Center for the Teaching and Learning of Literature at the State University of New York at Albany; Melanie Sperling; Jim Wertsch; and colleagues at Wisconsin: Deborah Brandt, Stuart Greene, Alison King, David Noskin, David Schaafsma (now at Columbia), Michael Smith (now at Rutgers), and Richard Young.

Special thanks to Colette Daiute and Robert Gundlach, who saw this project unfold in a series of presentations and symposia at the conventions of the American Educational Research Association and the National Council of Teachers of English, and who offered generous and incisive comments and unswerving support for the numerous drafts of the papers that became this book.

My editors at Teachers College Press, Carol Chambers Collins, Susan Alkana, and Lyn Grossman, provided expert advice on making a complicated and technical study accessible to a wide range of readers.

Needless to say, I and my collaborators are responsible for any oversights, inaccuracies, or misinterpretations that may remain.

My family, including my wife, Nancy, and our sons, Steve and Tim, have taught me my most important lessons about the role of close interaction and discourse in personal learning. This book is dedicated to Timothy Nystrand. To all my friends, colleagues, and family who have supported this work in ways too many to count, thank you.

Martin Nystrand

Opening Dialogue

UNDERSTANDING THE DYNAMICS OF LANGUAGE AND LEARNING IN THE ENGLISH CLASSROOM

All teachers' and students' names are pseudonyms.

CHAPTER 1

Dialogic Instruction: When Recitation Becomes Conversation

Martin Nystrand

Ms. Lindsay is writing on the board, trying hard to keep up with John, one of her students in this ninth-grade class, who has just read aloud his plot summary for a chapter from Mildred Taylor's *Roll of Thunder, Hear My Cry.*

"I had a lot of trouble," says Ms. Lindsay, "getting everything down [on the board], and I think I missed the part about trying to boycott." She reads from the board: "'and tries to organize a boycott.' Did I get everything down, John, that you said?"

"What about the guy who didn't really think these kids were a pest?" replies John.

"Yeah, okay," says Ms. Lindsay. "What's his name? Do you remember?" John shakes his head, indicating he can't remember.

Without waiting to be called on, Alicia, another student, volunteers, "Wasn't it Turner?"

Looking around the class, Ms. Lindsay says, "Was it Turner?" Several students say, "Yes."

"Okay," continues Ms. Lindsay, "so Mr. Turner resisted white help. Why? Why would he want to keep shopping at that terrible store?"

John quickly answers, "There was only one store to buy from because all the other ones were white."

"Well," Ms. Lindsay objects, "the Wall Store was white too."

Another student, Tom, now addressing John, wonders, "Is it Mr. Hollings's store? Is that it?"

"No," John answers. "Here's the reason. They don't get paid till the cotton comes in. But throughout the year they still have to buy stuff— food, clothes, seed, and stuff like that. So the owner of the plantation will sign for what they buy at the store so that throughout the year they can still buy stuff on credit."

"So," Ms. Lindsay says, reading aloud what she puts up on the board, "he has to have credit in order to buy things, and this store is the only one that will give it to him."

Another student, Felice, speaks up. "I was just going to say, it was the closest store."

Barely looking away from the board now, Ms. Lindsay replies while continuing to flesh out the paragraph building on the board, "Okay — it's the closest store; it seems to be in the middle of the area; a lot of sharecroppers who don't get paid cash — they get credit at that store — and it's very hard to get credit at other stores. So it's going to be very hard for her to organize that boycott; she needs to exist on credit.

"Yeah?" she says as she then nods to yet another student. Discussion continues.

In the 2 years that my colleagues and I visited hundreds of eighth- and ninth-grade literature classrooms, this brief excerpt of classroom discourse came to represent the most important qualities we found of instruction that works: that is, instruction that helps students understand literature in depth, remember it and relate to it in terms of their own experience, and — most important for literature instruction — respond to it aesthetically, going beyond the who, what, when, and why of nonfiction and literal comprehension (see Chapter 2). In this classroom, students were engaged, not merely "on task." Unlike most, this class was not about the transmission and recitation of information, and the teacher's role was not that of asking questions to see how much students knew and going over the points they did not yet understand. This session was about figuring things out — in class, face-to-face, teacher and students together.

Traditional teacher and learner roles here were reversed. Rather than lecturing or quizzing students about the main points, this teacher instead took notes from them about their ideas. There was no penalty for error in this class; feigning a lapse, the teacher allowed a student to help her with a character's name. In this class, students as well as the teacher asked key questions, and in the end it was the students, not the teacher, who explained the main point.

Most instruction is about what is already known and figured out. Indeed, learning and being prepared for class typically mean reliably remembering what is already known. This class went further, and instruction here was ultimately about working collaboratively to understand what was not yet understood. Clearly this teacher took her students seriously, and clearly they knew it. Instruction of this sort is described inadequately by the main points in a lesson plan. Capturing instruction and learning of this sort requires constructing a narrative of unfolding understandings involving thoughtful interaction between and among teacher and students.

This kind of instruction, we also learned, is rare in American schools. The rhetoric and conceptual apparatus of current thinking about curriculum and instruction make it easy to be seduced into believing that instruction is improving. Big ideas and big names from sociocultural theory are alive and well at all the major conferences. Whole language and workshop approaches are more popular than ever as topics of presentations, articles, and books. Yet despite an apparent emerging consensus about the sociocultural foundations and character of literacy and classroom discourse, most schooling is organized, we found, for the plodding transmission of information through classroom recitation. Teachers talk and students listen. And the lower the track, we found, the more likely this is to be true.

American high schools are all too often "orderly but lifeless" (Goodlad, 1984; Powell, Farrar, & Cohen, 1985; Sizer, 1984). Teachers tend to avoid controversial topics, simplifying complex issues into bite-sized pieces of information distilled into countless worksheets and continual recitation. These teachers maintain control through dull, plodding coverage of content. In response, students tend to do their work but show little enthusiasm for learning, and their work is often superficial, mindless, and quickly forgotten. In the classes we observed, only about a quarter of the students participated in question-and-answer recitation, and actual discussion of the sort examined above occurred, on average, less than one minute a day. Indeed, as we will see in Chapter 2, in the vast majority there was none at all. Almost all teachers' questions, moreover, required students to recall what someone else thought, not to articulate, examine, elaborate, or revise what they themselves thought. Let's consider an example.

In the following session, Mr. Schmidt reviews main points about *The Iliad* so that his ninth-grade students will have some basic understanding of plot, setting, and narrative.

"According to the poet," Mr. Schmidt asks, "what is the subject of *The Iliad*?"

Mary's hand goes up. "Achilles' anger," she answers when Mr. Schmidt calls on her.

But this is not the answer Mr. Schmidt is looking for. He pauses, then asks a more constrained question: "Where does the action of the first part of Book I take place when we enter the story?"

Mary does not raise her hand this time, but, after a long pause, Joshua tries, "On the Achaean ship?"

But this is not what Mr. Schmidt is after either. "Well," he says, "they're not on their ships. Let's see if we can give you a little diagram."

Corrine thinks she is catching on. "Was it on the shore?" she asks.

"Yes, it's on the shore," Mr. Schmidt says. "Let's see if we can kind of visualize where everything is here." He proceeds to draw on the board. "Remember that Troy is on the coast of Turkey—at the time called Asia Minor—so let's see if we can—okay—this is the scene, and all of the ships are anchored—a thousand ships are anchored here—Helen, the face that launched a thousand ships. So they are on the shore here, and this is the plains of Troy, a great city, and here's Troy, the great walled city. There's a big gate here. Now this is quite a few miles; it's a large plain. And the wall surrounds the city, and inside the city there are farms and whatever there is. The city can exist for a long time without ever having to go out. And periodically the Trojans come out and engage the Achaeans in battle. And at the end of the day, they go back home. They can't fight at night—they can't see anything; it's too dark. What's the point—you might be killing one of your friends—it's hard to tell one man from another. And very often if the Trojans don't feel like coming out to fight, they don't. . . . So the war has been going on now for how long?"

Hannah says, "Ten years."

Mr. Schmidt echoes Hannah, muttering "Ten years," and moves on. "You have to understand—the battle takes place only during the daytime." He then draws some more on the board. "So this is approximately what it looked like," pointing to his sketch. "Now the city is immense—much larger probably than what we consider the area of our own city; it could be as large as all of the county."

Lamar asks, "And the wall ran completely around it?"

"Yes," Mr. Schmidt says.

Joshua then asks, "Didn't they put a wall up in Ireland?"

"In Ireland?" Mr. Schmidt replies. "I'm not familiar with that." Moving the class back on track, he continues, "So, let's take a look at some of the other questions. What's the story behind the quarrel—it deals with Achilles and Briseis and Agamemnon and Chryses and Chryses's daughter Chryseis and how Agamemnon takes Chryseis away from Achilles to replace the prize Chryseis, who has gone back to her father. What is the result of the quarrel between Agamemnon and Achilles?"

Hannah has her hand raised, and Mr. Schmidt calls on her. "He's not going to participate in the battle anymore," she says.

Once again, Mr. Schmidt echoes Hannah, "He's not going to participate in the battle anymore," and then moves on, "What's the common custom of Greek warfare and prizes?"

Without raising his hand, Thomas begins to say, "That the prizes that they get. . .," but Mr. Schmidt goes on before he can finish. "What is Achilles' heritage?" he asks. "How does he use that power?"

There is no answer. Mr. Schmidt tries again: "How does he use the power that his mother is a goddess?"

Once again, there is no answer. After a few moments, he asks insistently, "What is the relationship between gods and men in the *Iliad*?"

It is Joshua this time. "Gods usually have power over the men no matter what."

"Okay," Mr. Schmidt acknowledges. "What else? What are some other parts of this relationship?"

Mary raises her hand. "When men give offerings when they pray."

"Okay," Mr. Schmidt says, indicating that the class is making progress, "a close, kind of a cause-and-effect relationship — you know if I do this for you I expect you to do something for me. What else? Do gods intervene in human affairs?"

"Yes," say both Hannah and Lamar.

"Specifically," replies Mr. Schmidt. "Where is an example?"

What is most striking about this recitation is the extent to which the teacher controls the discourse. Although the term *recitation* usually refers to students' oral presentation of previously learned material, this excerpt demonstrates how completely the teacher can do the actual reciting. The students play a minor and supporting role in what gets said here, mainly by responding with an occasional word or two to the teacher's periodic questions. Not always knowing whether their responses will be acceptable, they frequently hesitate; they develop no ideas of their own; they do a lot of guessing. This is a tightly scripted lesson; we get the impression that the teacher is working from a highly wrought list of topics and questions, covering particular points in a particular order (and perhaps preparing students for a test); that he has done so in the past and will do so again in the future; and that the makeup of each class affects the script very little. There is minimal interaction here between teacher and students.

It so happens that Mr. Schmidt's lesson eventually went on to something more interpretive soon after this episode. After class, he explained to us that he had deliberately quizzed students on these details of *The Iliad* as a way of "getting the facts on the table" so that the class could engage in an intelligent discussion of more interesting questions. This was his lead-in to discussing "what picture about life on Mount Olympus emerges from Book I." Many teachers in fact use recitation in just this way, and much classroom discourse, as we will examine in Chapter 2, manifests a rhythm of recitation and lecture, and sometimes includes more open-ended discussion. Most does not, however, and discussion was remarkably rare in the many classes we visited.

Recitation is by far the predominant mode of classroom discourse in American secondary schools, where it has been an idiosyncratic part of schooling for well over a century. In a 1908 study contrasting American and European pedagogy, Burstall (1909) found that European teachers mainly used lecture to "build up new knowledge in class," whereas American teachers, more focused on textbooks, tended to serve as "[chairmen] of a meeting, the object of which is to ascertain whether [students] have studied for themselves in a textbook" (Burstall, 1909, pp. 156, 158). The Americans prided themselves on their belief that recitations were more "democratic" than lectures because they potentially gave every student a chance to participate in lessons.

As we can see from the example above, this participation is carefully constrained. The teacher asks a series of typically unrelated questions in order to assess how much students know and do not know, as well as to check completion of assigned work and to reinforce key points. Student responses often are abbreviated and tentative — as often as not questions are answered with questions — as students try to figure out what the teacher is thinking or what someone else thought, not what they themselves think. The essential purpose of recitation, along with seatwork and study questions, is to transmit information to students and review it with them. Therefore, the teacher rarely follows up on student answers except when they are wrong, and 20% of all questions require only yes/no answers (Tharp & Gallimore, 1988, p. 14).[1] When recitation starts, remembering and guessing supplant thinking.

Listless classrooms are sometimes attributed to problems of motivation, methods, and curriculum, and no doubt many are. Yet for too long now, debates about curriculum and instruction and mental life in classrooms have been polarized by debates about which is better: teacher control or student control, direct instruction or collaborative learning. Indeed, a long tradition of research and polemic pitting of teacher versus student as the appropriate theoretical center for understanding curriculum and instruction has precluded our understanding that more basic than either teacher or student is *the relationship between them*. Lifeless instruction and reluctant student engagement and thinking may be viewed as fundamental problems of instructional discourse — of the kind of language that defines students' interactions with their teachers, peers, and texts. Instruction is "orderly but lifeless" when the teacher predetermines most of its content, scope, and direction.

In other, far fewer, secondary classrooms — like Ms. Lindsay's — teachers engage their students in more probing and substantive interactions, and the talk is more like conversation or discussion than recitation (Nystrand & Gamoran, 1991a, 1991b). In these classrooms, the teacher validates particular students' ideas by incorporating their responses into subsequent questions, a process Collins (1982) calls "uptake." In the give-and-take of such talk, students' responses and not just teacher questions shape the course of talk. The discourse in these classrooms is therefore less predictable and repeatable because it is "negotiated" and jointly determined — in character, scope, and direction—by both teachers and students as teachers pick up on, elaborate, and question what students say (Nystrand, 1990a, 1991a). Such interactions often are characterized by "authentic" questions, which are asked to get information, not to see what students know and do not know; that is, authentic questions are questions without "prespecified" answers (Nystrand & Gamoran, 1991a). These questions convey the teacher's interest in students' opinions and thoughts. Hence, in contrast to the "test questions" of recitation, or what Mehan (1979a) calls "known information questions," they indicate the priority the teacher places on thinking and not just remembering. These "instructional conversations," as Tharp & Gallimore (1988) call them, or "substantive conversations," as Newmann (1990) calls them, engage students because they validate the importance of students' contributions to learning and instruction. The purpose of such instruction is not so much the transmission of information as the interpretation and collaborative co-construction of understandings. In this kind of classroom talk, teachers take their students seriously (Gamoran & Nystrand, 1992).

Of course, instruction often falls somewhere between these two extremes of recitation on the one hand and discussion on the other. It is not uncommon for teachers to review essential points of information as a way of establishing a topic or issue that can then be discussed more interpretively. Discussions can sometimes "downshift" into review as this becomes necessary. We must be careful, too, not to define pedagogical engagement in terms of either how much students actually talk or how much time they spend on a given task, that is, time-on-task, a frequent measure of student engagement. The usefulness of such talk or time can be assessed only when the nature of the talk or task is considered. On the one hand, lectures can be useful when they respond to, anticipate, and/or engender curiosity and important student questions. On the other hand, many lively discussions are not really so free-formed but, like recitation, can be orchestrated by "right" answers, hidden agendas, and preordained conclusions. All of these complications make it clear that, in the final analysis, the key features of effective classroom discourse cannot be defined only by identifying particular linguistic forms such as question types, or even the genre of classroom discourse (lecture, discussion, etc.).[2] Ultimately the effectiveness of instructional discourse is a matter of the quality of teacher–student interactions and the extent to which students are assigned challenging and serious epistemic roles requiring them to think, interpret, and generate new understandings.

DIALOGISM: A FEW PRELIMINARIES

The work of early-twentieth-century Russian scholar Mikhail Bakhtin is useful for understanding how verbal interactions shape the understandings and thinking of the conversants. Bakhtin was a philosopher and literary theorist whose work recently has become a focus of great interest to researchers in language, literacy, composition, literature, and many other fields. Together with colleagues, including Vološinov, the "Bakhtin Circle" focused on how dialogue shapes both language and thought, and the perspective inspired by him (still very much under development) has come to be called *dialogism*.[3] Utterances were interesting to Bakhtin because he saw that they respond to previous utterances at the same time that they anticipate future responses. In this view, discourse is continuously woven into a "chain of speech communication" by one speaker's "responsive position" relative to another's. For Bakhtin, even long texts such as books are ultimately parts of extended dialogues involving perhaps other texts but always other voices of all kinds. In other words, Bakhtin's utterance is akin to what we now call a conversation turn. (Goodwin, 1981; Sacks, Schegloff, & Jefferson, 1974).

> Any utterance — from a short (single-word) rejoinder in everyday dialogue to the large novel or scientific treatise — has, so to speak, an absolute beginning and an absolute end: its beginning is preceded by the utterances of others, and its end is followed by the responsive utterances of others. (Bakhtin, 1986, p. 72)

Yet discourse is dialogic not because the speakers take turns, but because it is continually structured by tension, even conflict, between the conversants, between self and other, as one voice "refracts" another. It is precisely this tension — this relationship between self and other, this juxtaposition of relative perspectives and struggle among competing voices — that for Bakhtin gives shape to all discourse and hence lies at the heart of understanding as a dynamic, sociocognitive event.

A dialogic perspective on discourse and learning starts with the premise, then, that discourse is essentially structured by the interaction of the conversants, with each playing a particular social role. Instructional discourse is shaped by classroom participation structures and authority relationships (Gutierrez, 1992, 1993; Schultz, Erickson, & Florio, 1982) and by the extent of reciprocity between teachers and students (Nystrand & Gamoran, 1991a). This is why Ms. Lindsay initiates something far more intricate and reflective when she says, "Did I get everything down, John, that you said?" than what ensues when Mr. Schmidt asks his class, "According to the poet, what is the subject of *The Iliad*?" Mr. Schmidt's "faceless" test question is unaffected by who is attending class, and the class' superficial participation, as evidenced by their hesitant responses, is no doubt related to the underlying premise in this class that the content of literature is autonomous, "in the text," and unrelated to students' efforts aside from their correctly decoding "it." By contrast, Ms. Lindsay's question focuses the thinking of one particular student, but his engagement spreads to peers, who chip in their own ideas to help figure out why Turner kept shopping at "that terrible store." Her class operates on the premises (a) that the content of literature is not autonomous but has to be constructed by readers in engaged encounters with the text, and (b) that understandings are focused by struggles over meaning. Mr. Schmidt explains the text; Ms. Lindsay coaches her students in how to read and interpret literature.

Lotman (1988) claims that all language can be treated both dialogically and "univocally." When utterances are treated univocally, as in recitation, focus is on the "accurate transmission of information"; when they are treated dialogically, as in discussion, they are used as "thinking devices." Wertsch and Toma (1990) argue that the key instructional issue here is not whether language can ever be inherently dialogic or univocal, but rather whether teachers treat source texts, students' utterances, and their own statements as either "thinking devices" or a means for transmitting information. In other words, what counts is how teachers organize instruction. According to Barnes (1976; Barnes & Schemilt, 1974), transmission-oriented instructors like Mr. Schmidt view their function as providing information to students, whereas interpretation-oriented instructors like Ms. Lindsay view their function as stimulating students to go beyond right-and-wrong answers, especially in ways that gesture toward students' experience beyond the classroom. Wells (1993) defines the issue in terms of "the equality of participation by teachers and students in the processes of text creation" (p. 33).

The roles we establish as teachers and the interactions we undertake with our students, through our questions, responses, and assignments, inexorably set out the possibilities for meaning in our classes and, in this way, the context of learning. This is a fact of social organization. Whether we are teachers or students engaged in instruction, parents reading to our children, children teaching games to each other, motorists stopped by police, lovers sharing intimacies — whatever we say and think in these roles is shaped significantly by the social organization of the discourse and the respective roles of the conversants. A given utterance cannot be understood, Bakhtin/Medvedev (1985) writes,

> outside the organized interrelationships of the [conversants]. . . . The crux of the matter is not in the subjective consciousness of the speakers . . . or what [the speakers] think, experience, or want, but in *what the objective social logic of their interrelationships demands of them*. In the final account, this logic defines the very experiences of people (their "inner speech"). (p. 153; emphasis added)

That is to say, our relations with the significant others in our lives shape our consciousness — how we understand ourselves, others, and the world around us.[4] Even our most private thoughts — stream of consciousness, cryptic dialogues with ourselves, the ones that keep us awake at night — are ultimately reviews of and rehearsals for conversations with others. As Sperling (1991) eloquently writes, "The cognitive drama of one's composing processes is crowded with the often fleeting shadows of others" (p. 159).

Dialogism, then, is more than a theory of interaction. Because it offers insights into human interaction as a foundation of comprehension, meaning, and interpretation, it is of special interest to educators. What is special about Bakhtin and Vološinov is the way they derive an epistemology from a conception of social interaction, relating how people make sense of things to how they interact with each other. Bakhtin believed that the meaning we give to an individual utterance always emerges in our response to and anticipation of other utterances; utterances relate to each other in much the way that questions and answers reciprocally reflect each other. As Wertsch (1985) explains, "The actual meaning of [Bakhtin's] 'word with a sidewards glance' is always partially determined by the voice it is answering, anticipating, or even striving to ignore" (p. 65). A dialogic perspective on instruction highlights the role that intersecting multiple voices play in individuals' learning and the development of their understandings.

Social theories of discourse often emphasize the stable, shared meanings that bind and inform the behavior of individual members of groups. Learning is frequently characterized by such theories as the socialization of novices into these shared values and beliefs. Bakhtin's account of discourse differs from such theories by stressing interaction and the role of conflict, focusing on the dynamic processes whereby meanings unfold in the interaction of two or more conversants.[5]

THE SOCIAL LOGIC OF RECIPROCITY AND THE CONTINGENCY OF UTTERANCES

At the heart of Bakhtin's social logic is a reciprocity of roles: that is, the roles of teacher and learner (and parent and child, writer and reader, cop and speeder, lover and loved, etc.) each respectively and mutually entail those of the other, the one in effect defining the parameters of meaning and communication of the other.[6] Social phenomenologist Alfred Schutz (1967) regards this reciprocity as a transcendent social fact, explaining it by saying it is "assumed that the sector of the world taken for granted by me is also taken for granted by you, and even more, that it is taken for granted by 'Us'" (p. 12). This is why ostensibly individual acts such as mailing a letter (Schutz, 1967), writing (Nystrand, 1986), reading (e.g., Tierney, 1983; Tierney & LaZansky, 1980), and learning and cognitive development (Bruner, 1966; Vygotsky, 1978; Wertsch, 1979, 1985) are nonetheless social; each is premised on appropriate and respective acts by reciprocal others (postal workers for letter writers, readers for writers, writers for readers, teachers for learners). As

Brandt (1990) puts it, "Literacy is not a matter of learning to go it alone with language but learning to go it alone with each other" (p. 6).

In these terms, what we think and how we understand our experience always depends on how we respond to others at the same time that we anticipate their responses.[7] For Vološinov (1973):

> [W]ord is a two-sided act. It is determined equally by whose word it is and for whom it is meant. As word, it is precisely the product of the reciprocal relationship between speaker and listener, addresser and addressee. . . . I give myself verbal shape from another's point of view, ultimately from the point of view of the community to which I belong. A word is a bridge thrown between myself and another. . . . A word is territory shared by both addresser and addressee. (p. 86; emphasis in original)

This concept of discourse is fundamentally different from the common view that utterances are the independent expressions of thoughts by speakers, an account that starts with thoughts and ends with words and verbal articulation. Rather, because they respond to at the same time that they anticipate other utterances, they are "sequentially contingent" upon each other.[8] Thoughts, Bakhtin contends, are never simply "garbed," or wrapped in words, by an active speaker/writer for expression, transmission, and reception by a passive listener/reader. Rather, understandings evolve—are co-constructed—in "the unique interaction between author and reader, the play of two consciousnesses" (Bakhtin/Medvedev, 1985, p. 128).

Since learning is significantly shaped by learners' interactions, plus the responses they anticipate from teachers, peers, and texts, a key issue concerns the dialogic potential of different kinds of instructional discourse for learning. Is all instruction equally dialogic? In recitation, for example, the teacher's voice is so dominant that such instruction seems arguably far more "monologic" than dialogic. Teachers in recitation often change topics abruptly as soon as they are satisfied with students' mastery of a particular point, and they follow up student responses mostly to evaluate them, not to elaborate student ideas. By contrast, discussion is defined by the character of its tightly interlaced comments and responses.

Yet can we validly claim that some instruction is more dialogic than others? After all, isn't the fundamental premise of dialogism that all language is dialogic, even discourse we might be inclined to call monologic? Even in recitation, aren't students responding to teachers' questions? Isn't this interaction? Bakhtin addressed this issue first in his discussion of authoritative, official discourse. During the 1930s, when the Writers' Union announced that all Soviet writers were expected to write "fixed-form," "party-minded" social-realist novels (see Clark & Holquist, 1984), Bakhtin published The Dialogic Imagination (1981), contending that novels by definition can have no

fixed form since they are quintessentially novelists' orchestrations of competing voices, demonstrating what he called "heteroglossia" (many voicedness).
More generally, he argued, the language and discourse of any given time and
place are continuously shaped and pulled in different directions by interacting
forces of stability and change. On the one hand are the "centripetal" forces of
stability and canonization—rules of grammar, usage, "official genres," "correct" language, privileged ideologies; on the other hand are the "centrifigual"
forces of life, experience, and the natural pluralism of language. Hence, established public "authoritative discourse" is perpetually in conflict with the "innerly persuasive discourse" of the individual; to varying degrees they resist
and subvert each other. The history of language and literature, he claimed, is
replete with regular efforts to resist, censor, and suppress the forces of heteroglossia in the interests of stability and canonization; as an example, he cited
the Russian Orthodox Church seeking to impose a "single language of truth."[9]
Such authoritative, official discourse monologically resists communication,
seeking to extinguish competing voices and all differences between the group
and the individual. "Monologism, at its extreme," Bakhtin (1984) writes,

> denies the existence outside itself of another consciousness with equal rights and
> responsibilities. . . . Monologue is finalized and deaf to the other's response, does
> not expect it and does not acknowledge in it any *decisive* force. . . . Monologue
> pretends to be the *ultimate word*. (pp. 292–293; emphasis in original)

Holquist (1990) characterizes such discourse as "totalitarian"—"autism for
the masses" (p. 34). Yet such efforts to impose a contrived monologism, Bakhtin argued, inevitably must fail since discourse is inherently dialogic.[10]

STRIVING FOR MONOLOGISM

Although classroom discourse, like novels, can never be truly monologic,
it can be organized and treated as though it were. Teachers regularly strive for
monologism when, for example, they "prescript" both the questions they ask
and the answers they accept, as well as the order in which they ask the questions. Furthermore, teachers control discussions by the topics they allow to
be formulated and the "off-topics" they ignore (Eder, 1982). Recitation is
tightly structured according to a pedagogical contract that Mehan (1979b)
calls IRE, for teacher *initiation* (question), student *response*, and teacher *evaluation*. By evaluating student answers rather than responding to student comments and ideas, teachers effectively thwart dialogue by "control[ling] or curtail[ing] the nature of audience participation in any ongoing exchange"
(Drew & Heritage, 1992, p. 27). Through this "banking" method of instruc-

tion, Freire (1970) claims, teachers seek to "fill students up" with all the "essential" points and all the "right" answers, and it is this content that defines the authoritative discourse of the classroom. Like all official discourse, of course, such instruction inevitably fails to mute the inherent "multivoicedness" of the classroom, which continually resists the authoritative to varying degrees. As Dyson (1989) shows, students' unofficial voices assert themselves through glances and notes, and as Daiute and Griffin (1993) point out, students frequently construct "innerly persuasive" narratives to digest what they learn. Kachur and Prendergast (see Chapter 3) treat what is commonly characterized as "off-task" student behavior as a subversion of the authoritative, official discourse of the classroom. The dialogic in such classrooms persists despite the fact that instruction in such classrooms, like the efforts of the Soviet Writer's Union of the 1930s or Bakhtin's example of the Russian Orthodox Church, is monologically organized.

Composition instructors inculcate monologism to the extent that they promote the idea that written texts are "autonomous" documents having meaning apart from both the writer and readers. Historically, teachers have done this by defining sentences as statements of "complete ideas" and by promoting an objective (third-person) diction eschewing references to both the writer (*I*) and the reader (*you*). In his influential paper, "From Utterance to Text: The Bias of Language in Speech and Writing," David Olson (1977) perpetuated this fallacy by arguing that the meaning of written texts, unlike spoken utterances, resides entirely in texts independently of both writers and readers. Texts are "like Popeye," he claimed: They "*say*" what they *mean* and *mean* precisely, neither more nor less than, what they *say*" (Olson, 1981, p. 108; emphasis in original). Arguing for a kind of strict constructionism of text meaning, he went on to contend that, because texts, unlike utterances, are inherently "explicit," readers should only passively "decode" them, not actively interpret them; if readers allow any part of their prior knowledge or personal experience to give meaning to the text, "we charge . . . the reader with misreading the text" (Olson, 1977, p. 272).

This attempt to control text meaning by excluding the reader—and in the classroom, of course, this means students—from any role in its meaning represents an extreme monologism. It is also a premise whose validity has been soundly refuted over the last 2 decades. The reading process now is commonly understood, for example, as readers' active construction of meaning from text cues (Smith, 1971), and anyone who might read without making critical and strategic use of prior knowledge is treated as having either a basic reading disorder or a deficit in cultural literacy (Hirsch, 1987), or both. From research on writing (e.g., Nystrand, 1987), we know that explicitness and elaborateness of text are totally unrelated to fullness of meaning, which is why cryptic texts such as STOP and EXIT signs are usually more explicit than

painfully elaborate IRS documents and life insurance policies. For both writing and talk, moreover, meaning is equally and critically dependent on the
context of their use — this is true not only for EXIT signs, which make sense
only next to doors, but also for essays, which make full sense only when read
in the context of a particular debate or forum of inquiry. As I have previously
argued, a text is explicit not because it says everything all by itself but rather
because it strikes a careful balance between what needs to be said and what
may be assumed: The writer's problem "is not just being explicit; The writer's
problem is knowing what to be explicit about" (Nystrand, 1986, p. 81).
Brandt (1990) shows how texts are as much about reading as they are about
content: "Texts talk incessantly about the acts of writing and reading in progress. . . . What they refer to is not an explicit message but the implicit process
by which intersubjective understanding is getting accomplished" (p. 4). Indeed, even Olson (1991) has abandoned all defense of his doctrine of autonomous texts, recently arguing:

> Now, finally, is textual meaning really autonomous? I would acknowledge that it
> is not. Texts are always open to re-interpretation. . . . Not only do their meanings
> change as contexts change but also the textual or sentence meanings change as
> cultural conventions change. So there is no absolute meaning of a text. Nor is
> there one true intention of which a text is a fragmentary expression. (p. 19)

If a new consensus among researchers affirms that all discourse — not just
conversation but also writing — is categorically dialogic, the message has
largely been lost on the schools, however. Cazden (1988) argues that schools
continue to focus on decontextualized skill exercises and engage students in
writing tasks independent of any actual communicative context. How are we
to explain this discrepancy between what seems to be the case about discourse
and what seems to be the case about instruction? The only way to understand
this paradox, Cazden contends, is to view the doctrine of autonomous text as
a prevailing myth: a contention of dubious validity that nonetheless sustains
and "justifies decontextualized exercises for the practice of generic skills of
explicitness" (p. 120). In short, although all discourse is inherently dialogic,
it can be treated — and regularly is — as though it were monologic. This is
how many teachers — whether in recitation or in the doctrine of autonomous
texts — strive for monologism in the classroom.

In monologically organized instruction, the main loss is that, when teachers make no public classroom space for student voices — no "ample space for
'unofficial worlds'" within the "official world" of the school, as Dyson (1993,
p. 19) puts it — they miss many "teachable moments" by not responding to
their students in timely, fortuitous ways. As Rosen (1992) argues, "It is necessary to insist again and again on the need to disrupt the authoritative voice
with the unheard voices of our students, to help them engage in the diffi-

cult struggles . . . to articulate, develop, refine and advance their meanings as against the mere reproduction of words of the textbook, the worksheet, the encyclopedia and the guides" (p. 127, quoted in Cazden, in press). For example, in monologically organized instruction, the textbook and teacher's voice are the main voices, whereas in dialogically organized instruction, teachers make some public space for unofficial student voices; consequently, the discourse is more balanced so that the teacher's voice is but one voice among many, albeit a critical one.

The fundamental issues in a dialogic conception of instruction concern the scope of public classroom space for student voices and how various teacher roles and moves enhance, constrain, and otherwise affect the interpretive roles and therefore the learning of students. Key questions include:

- How does classroom discourse define what counts as knowledge in a given class?
- How does the public arrangement of classroom discourse establish and sustain epistemic roles like remembering and thinking, and how in turn do these affect learning?
- How do students manage these roles?
- What characterizes the chains of understanding that teachers initiate and sustain with their students?
- How can teachers organize classroom discourse to enhance their students' learning?

Questions such as these are the central focus of the study reported in this and the following chapters.

CLASSROOM CONTRACTS AND THE TERMS OF LEARNING

As we examine the organization of instruction, we discover that pedagogical "contracts"—what Powell, Farrar, and Cohen (1985) call "treaties" between teachers and students, and what Gutierrez (1991) calls "instructional scripts"—vary greatly and that their character significantly affects student learning. These instructional arrangements, Gutierrez (1992) shows, determine discourse patterns, rules of participation, and the nature of classroom interaction. In too many classrooms, Powell, Farrar, and Cohen (1985) tell us, teachers essentially agree not to demand too much, and students more or less agree to comply. As we have seen, such classes typically are devoted to the accurate transmission and recall of information and are largely characterized by lecture, recitation, seatwork, worksheets, study questions, and tests. In recitation, the teacher, following a prescribed checklist of questions, information, and concepts, sticks closely to a preplanned list of test questions rather than responding to the substance of what students say (Nystrand & Gamoran, 1991a). Students typically give short, frequently tentative answers (Nystrand, 1991a). Topic shifts can be abrupt as the teacher moves down a checklist of important points, as it were, making sure students remember them. As a result, the discourse frequently is choppy and lacks coherence — it is "the oral equivalent of short-answer questions and filling in blanks" (Nystrand, 1991b, p. 7). Carlsen (1991) speculates that teachers control discourse topics and student participation by manipulating the pace of questioning and the time they wait before asking subsequent questions, keeping discussion "on target," for example, through fast-paced questioning. The participation structure in these classrooms, so completely dominated by the teacher and text, is one-sided and monologic. Students respond to teachers' questions, but teachers, more often than not, respond only by moving on to the next question. Indeed, the very structure of recitation effectively serves to thwart dialogue by "control[ling] or curtail[ing] the nature of audience participation in any ongoing exchange" (Drew & Heritage, 1992, p. 27). As Heath (1978) and others note, student participation is mainly procedural (see also Bloome, Puro, & Theodorou, 1989; Moll, 1990; Nystrand & Gamoran, 1991a).

The contract underlying this unique three-part exchange, which exists only in instructional situations — including parent–child interactions in middle-class homes (Heath, 1983) — has several key provisions. First, knowledge is a given, and its source is the teacher or textbook, never students: The teacher prescripts and monitors all the answers. The teacher initiates all topics of discussion and determines what is worth knowing (defined as remembering). Knowledge is treated as fixed, objective, autonomous; for students it is given, transmitted, and received — what Rommetveit (1974) terms "stable concepts and referents" derived independently of students prior to class and typically compiled in lesson plans and curriculum guides. The epistemic role of students under the terms of such contracts is limited to remembering what others, especially teachers and textbooks, have said, not figuring things out (aside from which answers are correct) and not generating any new knowledge.

If students are to become substantively engaged, they must do more than comply with the procedures of classroom interaction. Freire (1970) claims that this happens best when teachers pose problems that students can, through critical thinking, relate to their own experience, in dialogic terms weaving their learning into a chain of utterances emanating from their lives. The result is "substantive engagement," a sustained commitment to and involvement with academic content and issues. In classes characterized by such engagement, recitation becomes something more like the conversation in Ms.

Lindsay's classroom, where teachers and students explore issues in depth. In dialogic instruction, there is more give-and-take between teachers and students, particularly concerning the substance of discussion. This is reciprocity. Students not only answer questions; they also make points and contribute to discussions. "In a good conversation," Britton (1970) once wrote, "the participants profit from their own talking . . . , from what others contribute, and above all from the interaction — that is to say, from the enabling effect of each upon the others" (p. 173). Compared with recitation, dialogic instruction involves fewer teacher questions and more conversational turns as teachers and students alike contribute their ideas to a discussion in which their understandings evolve. Unlike recitation, dialogic instruction is less pre-scripted since the actual conduct, direction, and scope of the discussion depend on what students as well as teachers contribute and especially on their interaction. As a result, dialogic instruction is more coherent, more sustained and in-depth, and more thematic than recitation.[11]

The terms of discourse contracts in these classrooms significantly involve thinking and grappling on the spot with new problems, including some the teacher may not have considered yet. Students may be sources of knowledge. Knowledge is something generated, constructed, indeed co-constructed in collaboration with others. Students figure out, not just remember. The teacher's role is to moderate, direct discussion, probe, foresee, and analyze the implications of student responses. Whereas knowledge in recitation is pre-scripted, knowledge during discussion unfolds, a process that values personal knowledge and accordingly promotes student ownership.

This is not to say that recitation is noninteractive. As noted earlier, the teacher asks questions, students make responses, and the teacher often evaluates the responses (see Lemke, 1988; Wells, 1993). Nor can we claim that such interactions are totally lacking in reciprocity. A more useful characterization is Heath's (1978) distinction between *procedural display* and *substantive engagement*. In procedural display, reciprocity is limited to classroom rules and regulations, and students seem mainly to be "doing school"; such instruction is characterized by choppy discourse and tentative, truncated student responses. Compared with the substantive engagement of discussion, which consists of conversation-like exchanges between the teacher and students and among peers, however, the interaction of recitation is superficial and procedural: Merely going through the motions of school, students quickly forget what they've learned. If we distinguish dialogically organized instruction as somehow more fully interactive than monologically organized instruction, interaction must be understood as more than a behavioral sequence or procedure in which one turn follows another. Such interaction between teacher and students also must configure (intermingle) or reconfigure the respective purposes and perspectives of the conversants; it must *effect a transformation of shared knowledge* (Nystrand, 1990b). That is, rather than filling students up with what they don't know, the focus is on starting with and expanding existing understandings. In these terms, recitation fails the test of dialogicality since it is based not on teachers and students actively sharing knowledge but rather on teachers reviewing the status of previous student knowledge. Discussion engenders discourse; recitation elicits a performance.

In its emphasis on reciprocity, contracts, and intersubjectivity, dialogism sometimes is misunderstood as a philosophy of untroubled egalitarianism in discourse — an "I'm okay — you're okay," happy, hopeful world where the conversants inevitably put aside their differences to revel in synch in an orgy of cooperation, mutuality, and untroubled assent. Yet Bakhtin teaches us that it is conflict, not harmony, that fuels response: The struggle of multiple, competing voices is the irreducible social fact of all discourse.[12] This is why monologically organized instruction, by seeking to suppress this diversity, risks disengaged, off-task students. As teachers, we know (as do our students) the inevitable dead end of assignments requiring students to explain things we already know — all those things our dialogically astute students know we know. Good students play along, of course, so that we can tell that they know that *we* know that *they* know what we know! Perfectly shared understanding precludes the need for authentic discourse; it is precisely this kind of lifeless, inauthentic discourse — dances with teachers, we might call it — that characterizes the most ineffective classrooms (Nystrand, 1993).

In Bakhtin's (1981) terms, dialogically organized instruction provides public space for student responses, accommodating and frequently intermingling teacher–student voices representing differing values, beliefs, and perspectives, and ideally including the voices of different classes, races, ages, and genders. Dialogically organized instruction is fueled by such pluralism and heteroglossia, and the extent of social interactiveness clearly shapes both instruction and learning. Monologically organized instruction such as the recitation in Mr. Schmidt's lesson occupies the low end of this dialogic continuum, whereas discussion and conversation-like discourse like Ms. Lindsay's occupy the high end. Recitation involves interaction that is superficial and procedural since it typically fails to affect the substance of the discourse, which is prescribed by the teacher. In dialogically organized instruction, teacher–student interaction extends to the substance of the discourse, so that multiple perspectives offered by teacher, students, and course readings all affect the shared understandings that the class collectively negotiates. Table 1.1 summarizes these distinctions between monologically organized and dialogically organized instruction.

Table 1.1. **Key Features of Monologically and Dialogically Organized Instruction**

	Monologically Organized Instruction	Dialogically Organized Instruction
Paradigm	Recitation	Discussion
Communication model	Transmission of knowledge	Transformation of understandings
Epistemology	Objectivism: Knowledge is a given	Dialogism: Knowledge emerges from interaction of voices
Source of valued knowledge	Teacher, textbook authorities: Excludes students	Includes students' interpretations and personal experience
Texture	Choppy	Coherent

HOW DISCOURSE SHAPES LEARNING

Let us return to the examples of classroom discourse at the start of this chapter to examine more closely how teacher–student interaction is related to student learning. A given discourse begins when the first conversant initiates a mutual frame of reference. In doing so, the initial conversant seeks to establish not only the topic of discourse but also her relationship with the other conversants and the scope of talk.[13] For example, Ms. Lindsay's initial question, "Did I get everything down, John, that you said?" establishes John's interpretation as the topic of discourse, and her role as coach in procedures for interpreting a literary text. Mr. Schmidt's initial question, "According to the poet, what is the subject of *The Iliad*?" establishes basic information about *The Iliad* as the topic of discourse, and his role as expert examiner.

The character of discourse in these lessons then unfolds as students respond to the respective questions and teachers respond to the students in turn. In Ms. Lindsay's class, student understandings become elaborated and fleshed out. In Mr. Schmidt's class, the monologic character of recitation precludes such development; no student ideas are elaborated. Students respond to his questions, but he does not follow up on anything they say. Indeed, when Mary replies that *The Iliad* is about "Achilles' anger," he responds by rephrasing his question to avoid anything so interpretive. "Where does the action of the first part of Book I take place?" he asks. Yet understandings develop, Bakhtin shows us, only when responses are sequentially contingent — teachers responding to students, not just students to teachers. Too often in recitation, the teacher moves on to the next question just as soon as a student demonstrates what she knows. This is one of the ways monologic instruction consistently short-circuits the development of ideas (Nystrand,

1991c). Depth of understanding requires elaboration of the learner's, not the teacher's, interpretive framework, and it is the important purpose of dialogic instruction to promote just such development. When teachers ask authentic questions — encouraging individual interpretations — they open the floor to student ideas for examination, elaboration, and revision. When teachers help students read literature on their own terms and values, reading also becomes authentic and helps students examine, elaborate, and revise their ideas. In Smith's (1971) terms, comprehension is enhanced when the teacher encourages students to work from a store of personal knowledge; in so doing, students are able more easily to predict the information of the text. Literature especially offers such possibilities since, as Rosenblatt (1938) shows, literature potentially enhances the fullness and quality of interactions between the world of the reader and the world of the text (see also Langer, 1995).

In the first example at the beginning of this chapter, Ms. Lindsay clearly establishes the dialogic character of instruction. She does this by taking notes from a student rather than, as is the more usual format, by making the points that students are expected to take down in notes of their own. It is precisely her responsiveness to John's ideas that permits their elaboration. Unlike typical recitation in which the teacher assesses how much students know, this lesson is more a discussion in which the teacher guides the students' investigation of a particular character's motivation. Hence, the teacher's evaluation of John's response here is high level and student centered. This is evident when Ms. Lindsay says, "I had a lot of trouble getting everything down [on the board], and I think I missed the part about trying to boycott. . . . Did I get everything down, John, that you said?" Here, the teacher's evaluation, implicit in her acting as class secretary for John's ideas, which she writes on the board, is high level because it validates John's ideas and puts them into the play of discussion. High-level evaluations often follow authentic questions; both are thinking devices by which teachers dialogically open the floor to student ideas.

In these ways, Ms. Lindsay and her students proceed to make sense of a topic — "the guy who didn't really think these kids were a pest" — that a student, not the teacher, has established. With classmates' help, this person is identified as Turner, and the teacher then moves to examine Turner's motivation for "shopping at that terrible store." John first suggests that "there was only one store to buy from because all the other ones were white," but the teacher objects that "the Wall Store was white too." After examining additional claims, the class finally arrives at an expanded understanding of this event.

Teachers often follow up student responses by elaborating important implications they see. Teachers sometimes turn some of these elaborations into didactic or instructive elucidations — little set pieces — of important points in a prescripted lesson plan that students should not miss. Others are more serious explorations of lines of inquiry opened up by students. When the latter occur, we may say that teacher evaluation is high level: The teacher notes the importance of a student's response in shaping a new understanding, and the course of interactions changes somewhat because of what the student has said. That is, evaluation is high when a student contributes something new to the discussion that modifies the topic in some way, and is so acknowledged by the teacher. Specifically, high-level evaluation consists of two parts.

1. The teacher's certification of the response (e.g., Ms. Lindsay: "I had a lot of trouble getting everything down [on the board], and I think I missed the part about trying to boycott.")
2. The teacher's incorporation of the response into the discourse of the class, usually in the form of either an elaboration (or commentary) or a follow-up question (e.g., "Did I get everything down, John, that you said?")

For level of evaluation to be high, the evaluation must be more than "Good," "Good idea," or a mere repeating of the student's answer. The teacher must push the student's contribution further, validating it in such a way that it affects the subsequent course of the discussion. When a teacher's evaluation is high level, the student really "gets the floor," as John does. Hence, high-level evaluation, like authentic questions, directly affects the dialogicality of teacher–student interaction.

In contrast to recitation, dialogic instruction results in mutual understandings worked out through class interaction. These discussions are often unique, reflecting the particular views and convictions of the mix of teacher and students in a given class; this is the reason teachers are sometimes surprised and puzzled to find they cannot repeat the same "hot" discussion with subsequent classes.[14] Although such discussions can seem at times highly inefficient ways of teaching — after all, couldn't Ms. Lindsay simply have explained quickly why Mr. Turner continued to shop at that same awful store? — dialogic instruction treats such interaction as an essential prerequisite to learning.

The following transcript of a ninth-grade English lesson on Mark Twain's *The Adventures of Huckleberry Finn* provides another example of dialogic instruction. In this review session, Ms. Turner elicits student responses to a series of questions about racism in the novel.

"Can you recall things from *Huck Finn* that, um, seemed racist to you?" Ms. Turner asks.

She calls on Tasha, who says, "Miss Watson's . . . that guy she's always calling 'Miss Watson's nigger.'"

"Okay. Jim?" Ms. Turner says.

"Well," he says, "they sell the slaves. . . . Also, they said in one part, 'Fetch in the nigger.'"

"Yeah," Ms. Turner says as Jim continues, "and it's like, you know, it's like you're saying to a dog, 'Here, boy.'"

"Right," Ms. Turner says, now recalling Twain's words: "'We fetched in the niggers to have prayers' — yeah, that's in probably the first couple of pages. Good. Sam?"

"Isn't [Twain] being historically accurate when he says 'those niggers'?" asks Sam.

"Oh, yes, absolutely," replies Ms. Turner.

Sam quickly asks, "So why is it racist?"

Pausing briefly, Ms. Turner says, "Well, this, that's kind of what I was trying to bring out on the first day, is that Twain is really just trying to mirror the society, and especially the society of . . . Missouri . . . at the time . . . but Twain is using the word rather sarcastically. I mean, you're right, he's being historically accurate, but he's also trying to make a point, um, about the different people who are saying things like that. How did that make you guys feel, I mean what was your gut reaction to all that? Linda?"

"Ashamed," says Linda.

"In what way?" asks Ms. Turner.

Linda continues. "That the one that it was for was . . . wanted to believe that it was something else."

Ms. Turner nods to Cassie, who has something to add. "Everyone claims it's so historical, you can find that anywhere . . . 'nigger,' you know, you just hear that . . . and people always think . . . it's so historical."

"Like, oh, we wouldn't do that anymore," Ms. Turner suggests.

"Yeah, like oh, we're not primitive," continues Cassie. "You know, and it's not, I mean, everybody does that, all the time. Well, not everybody, but people, people do that . . . people can't get in[to] apartment buildings because they're black."

"Um-hm," says Ms. Turner.

"They can't go to certain stores because they're black," Jim continues, "or they're arrested because they're black . . . you know, it's just, I mean, everybody is always saying how historical it is, and it's right here, and it's right now. . . ."

In all of the excerpts of ninth-grade literature instruction we have examined, the teachers seek to help students understand an important but complicated facet of the work they are teaching: Ms. Lindsay works on character motivation in *Roll of Thunder*, Mr. Schmidt teaches students details of Achaean–Trojan battle and the relationship of gods and men in *The Iliad*, and Ms. Turner focuses on racism in *The Adventures of Huckleberry Finn*. Each session elicits student recall.

Beyond this, however, Ms. Lindsay's and Ms. Turner's sessions differ from Mr. Schmidt's in important ways. Unlike Mr. Schmidt's test questions, the two women's questions are often authentic. Whereas Mr. Schmidt's first question is, "According to the poet, what is the subject of *The Iliad*?" Ms. Lindsay's first question concerns John's interpretation of character motivation, and Ms. Turner's first question is, "Can you recall things from *Huck Finn* that seemed racist to you?" In the last case, the teacher establishes the topic of discourse (racism in *Huck Finn*) and encourages students to treat it in their own terms. Hence, while the topic is the teacher's, many of the elaborations are the students'. The shared understandings that the latter two teachers achieve with their students are negotiated in the unfolding discourse of the class session. This dialogic process of co-construction is clearly evident in the fact that Ms. Lindsay's and Ms. Turner's students, unlike Mr. Schmidt's, are very active: Whereas the average student response in Mr. Schmidt's class is only about 5 words in length, responses in Ms. Turner's class average nearly 17 words.[15] Mr. Schmidt shifts topics with almost every question, whereas the other teachers sustain topics throughout the responses of several students; hence, topics in the latter two sessions receive multiple elaborations. Compared with the choppy nature of Mr. Schmidt's lesson, the other two lessons are far more coherent.

Mr. Schmidt's questions emphasize what Lotman (1988) calls the "univocal" function of *The Iliad;* hence, his main concern is reviewing basic information with students, who will need to recall it. The other two lessons, by contrast, have a more conceptual orientation (focusing on character motivation in the first, racism in the second), which is why Ms. Lindsay and Ms. Turner emphasize the dialogic function of their questions as well as student responses, treating student responses and comments in turn as "thinking devices," to use Lotman's (1988) term. Mr. Schmidt keeps students on a tight leash, as it were, holding them to "the facts." By contrast, the other teachers deliberately go out of their way to elicit and probe sustained student responses — indeed, this is precisely Ms. Turner's central purpose — and, by the end, each class's understanding of the respective novel is a co-construction. Instead of focusing on information to be received, encoded, and stored, Ms. Lindsay and Ms. Turner "take an active stance toward [what their students say] by questioning and extending [their utterances], by incorporating them into their own . . . utterances" (Wertsch & Toma, 1990, p. 13). For example, when John asks, "What about the guy who didn't really think these kids were a pest?" Ms. Lindsay turns the questions back on the class ("Yeah, okay.

What's his name? Do you remember?"). Ms. Turner, when asked if Twain wasn't "being historically accurate when he says 'those niggers,'" notes, "Well, this, that's kind of what I was trying to bring out on the first day, . . . that Twain is really just trying to mirror the society. . . . " Both Ms. Lindsay and Ms. Turner go to greater lengths than Mr. Schmidt to integrate students' responses into an unfolding understanding.

This is not to say, of course, that the discussions are totally freewheeling and unguided by the teacher. The teachers all move classroom talk in particular directions. Nonetheless, even when Ms. Turner alludes to points she made in previous classes ("That's kind of what I was trying to bring out on the first day"), it seems done less for the purposes of transmitting information (this session doesn't seem to be a review for a test) than to probe and elaborate an understanding of racism in *Huck Finn*.

If, in Mr. Schmidt's lesson, it is students who do little more than periodically chime in on cue to help him make his points, it is the other teachers who prop up and shepherd student elaborations into the mainstream of an unfolding discourse. The focus of Mr. Schmidt's lesson is a set of points he has prepared to make; the focus of the other classes is the process of interpreting the text and giving it meaning. For Mr. Schmidt, the meaning of the text is fixed and precedes the class hour; in Vološinov's (1976) terms, it is "finished off" independently of the students whose main task, in the view of the teacher, is to figure it out or, more accurately in this case, take it in as he explains it to them. Bakhtin (1984) specifically called such discourse "pedagogical dialogue."

> In an environment of . . . monologism the genuine interaction of consciousness is impossible, and thus genuine dialogue is impossible as well. In essence idealism knows only a single mode of cognitive interaction among consciousnesses: someone who knows and possesses the truth instructs someone who is ignorant of it and in error; that is, it is the interaction of a teacher and a pupil, which, it follows, can only be a pedagogical dialogue. (p. 81)

Epistemologically, knowledge in such pedagogical dialogues is treated as a given—completely objective, existing apart from the knowers (students) and prior to class.[16] Ms. Lindsay and Ms. Turner, by contrast, view reading as a meaning-making event in which students do not simply discover the meaning of the text but rather must interpret it in light of their own personal experience and expectations. They skillfully use classroom interaction not as a way to see whether students know the right answers, but rather as a way of instructing and rehearsing students in processes of interpretation. Instruction in these classes is based on the premise, as Bruner (1981) puts it, that actual meanings emanate not from abstract concepts or dictionary definitions but rather from an unfolding chain of references "whose last link is the present speaker" (p. 170). Knowledge here is partly what Polanyi (1958) called personal, involving investment in and commitment to valued beliefs and truths. Here the meaning of the text unfolds; it is not yet "finished off." By posing problems, these teachers act as midwives facilitating processes of interpretation. When a student says, with considerable hesitation, "Everyone claims it's so historical, you can find that anywhere . . . 'nigger,' you know, you just hear that . . . and people always think . . . it's so historical," the teacher helps by rephrasing, "Like, oh, we wouldn't do that anymore." Then a student, in turn, continues, "Yeah, like oh, we're not primitive. You know, and it's not, I mean, everybody does that, all the time. Well, not everybody, but people, people do that . . . people can't get in[to] apartment buildings because they're black." At this point, the discourse becomes fully conversational.

The contrast between these monologic and dialogic lessons is clarified still further when we examine the roles of the conversants in the discourse structure of each exchange. Consider, for example, the respective roles of teacher and students in initiating discourse topics, or what is talked about, and sustaining their elaboration. Mr. Schmidt's session is essentially a monologue, with the teacher responsible for both topics and elaborations; student comments are largely peripheral. By contrast, as noted above, the other two are more like conversations, with students elaborating a sizable share of the commentary; teacher and students share control over the discourse. The teacher's questions and comments frequently depend, moreover, on student responses, and vice versa. What particular students say affects the course of Mr. Schmidt's class very little, if at all, whereas the shape of the other two depends significantly on what students in those classes say.

In short, Mr. Schmidt's lesson differs from the others entirely in the respective roles of teacher and students. In his class, the teacher makes all the substantive points, while students' roles are limited to the procedural requirements of recitation; when called on, they try to provide the correct answers. By contrast, students in the other classes are expected to provide thoughtful answers based on their own experience, including their reading of the text. If recitation is organized to identify and correct what students do *not* know, dialogic instruction starts with what students *do* know or intuit (e.g., their understanding of racism), and progressively modifies and/or expands this understanding. As Bakhtin (1984) writes:

> The dialogic means of seeking truth is counterposed to *official* monologism, which pretends to *possess a ready-made truth*. . . . Truth is not born nor is it to be found inside the head of an individual person, it is born *between people* collectively searching for truth, in the process of their dialogic interaction. (p. 110; emphasis in original)

Whereas monologically organized instruction seeks to transmit information, dialogic instruction works by cultivating knowledge — transforming understandings through reflection and talk (Bickard, 1987).

Gutierrez (1991, 1992, 1993) argues that these different patterns of teacher–student interaction, which she calls "instructional scripts," define significantly different instructional contexts affecting (a) rules and rights of lesson participation, (b) the social hierarchy and relationships among teachers and students, and (c) epistemology, that is, whether knowledge is "precast" and transmitted by the teacher or dynamically co-constructed through classroom interaction. Gutierrez (1993) sums up the respective features of monologic recitation and dialogic exchanges, which she calls "responsive-collaborative script," as follows:

Recitation

Gutierrez (1993) summarizes the following features of recitation:

- Classroom talk follows strict IRE discourse pattern.
- Teacher selects student speakers.
- Teacher shows little or no acknowledgment of students' self-selections.
- Teacher initiates subtopics.
- Teacher discourages or ignores students' attempts to introduce other subtopics.
- Student responses tend to be short (one word/phrase); teacher does not encourage response elaboration, and there is minimal expansion of students' responses by teacher.
- Teacher initiates test-like questions for which there is generally only one correct answer and indicates implied goal is to contribute specific "right" answers to teacher's questions. (fig. 1)

Dialogic Exchange

Gutierrez (1993) discusses the following features of dialogic exchange, or, in her words, "responsive-collaborative script" (pp. 12–14):

- Activity and discourse boundaries are significantly relaxed with more student responses between teacher initiation and evaluation; also student responses occasionally build on previous responses (chained) and contribute to the construction of shared knowledge.
- Teacher frames and facilitates the activity and can respond at any time, but keeps utterances and intervention to a minimum.

- There is minimal teacher selection of students: Students either self-select or select other students.
- Teacher and students negotiate subtopics of discussion.
- Teacher indicates implied goal as developing shared knowledge, but still includes a preference for correct information.
- Teacher and students initiate questions for which there are no specific correct answers as well as questions that are constructed from students' previous responses.
- Teacher sometimes acknowledges students' topic expansions as well as teacher's and other students' incorporation of these expansions into the ongoing lesson.

Looking at teacher–student interaction in this way enables us to build on well-established findings that preschool children's language and cognitive development are conditioned by the language and social environment of their families. In research on preschool (emergent) literacy, for example, many studies have documented the indirect effects of a rich home discourse environment on developing literacy skills. These studies have examined the role of bedtime stories in the emergent literacy of young children (Heath, 1980); the contexts in which preschoolers explore interests in writing and reading (e.g., Bissex, 1980; Gundlach, 1982; Scollon & Scollon, 1980; Teale & Sulzby, 1986); the traditions and messages that parents transmit to their children about the uses of print (Heath, 1983); and the game interactions of parents and children (Wertsch & Hickmann, 1987). In school itself, we know that learning is readily undermined when some groups of students are marginalized by the academic life of the school. Consider, for example, the plight of urban Black students whose teachers often conclude from their African American English vernacular — fallaciously regarded as "ungrammatical" (Labov, 1969) — that they are unintelligent and unmotivated, and who are inauspiciously placed in remedial classes and vocational tracks as a result. Or consider the special difficulties that Mexicanos/as (immigrants raised in Mexico and now living in the United States) experience as they encounter and accommodate the expository language forms indigenous to middle-class American academics (Farr & Elías-Olivares, 1988). These many studies affirm that, in order to track and understand the path of writing development in individual children, it is not enough to track the evolution of written forms, norms, and textual features. Beyond these, researchers must focus more comprehensively on children's interactions with others, which is to say, on the social context of their learning, which sanctions their reading and writing and consequently promotes values and expectations that are essential to literacy.

WHY INTERACTIVE DISCOURSE PROMOTES LEARNING

Why, then, should dialogically organized instruction promote learning? First, both the character and tone of classroom discourse set important expectations for learning. As a genre of classroom discourse, for example, sustained classroom discussion validates students as important sources of knowledge and stimulates modes of cognition (thinking and not just remembering) that differ from those of recitation. Furthermore, when teachers ask questions about what students are thinking (and not just to see whether students have done their homework), and when they ask questions about students' previous answers, they promote fundamental expectations for learning by seriously treating students as thinkers, that is, by indicating that what students think is important and worth examining. Hence, the quality of classroom discourse is important because it establishes a suitable climate for learning and communicates teachers' expectations for their students' thinking.

Good discourse facilitates learning, moreover, by promoting students' engagement with their studies. When teachers ask students to explain their thinking and not just report someone else's, they treat each student as a primary source of information, thereby giving the students an opportunity to deal with things in their own frames of reference. Cognitive psychology has long known that learning is promoted when students can relate what they must learn to what they already know (Miller, 1956; Wittrock, 1990). It follows then that effective instruction will help students make the best use of what they already know. This is merely a way of saying that students learn best when instruction is coherent. Cognitively, this coherence benefits students because it increases the degree to which information is "thematized" and thereby promotes "chunking" of information (Miller, 1956), which, in recitation, too often tends to remain disparate and unrelated. Wittrock (1990; Wittrock & Alesandrini, 1990) shows that students' retention of new information is enhanced when they are able to relate it to their personal experience and especially when they do so in their own words. Pressley and his colleagues (Pressley, Wood, Woloshyn, Martin, King, & Menke, 1992) show that understanding and retention also are promoted by opportunities for self-generated elaborations. Discussion and interactive discourse promote learning because they elicit relatively sustained responses from students. By helping students weave various bits and pieces of information into coherent webs of meaning, dialogically organized instruction promotes retention and in-depth processing associated with the cognitive manipulation of information.

We may usefully categorize instructional discourse—writing, reading, and classroom talk—according to the extent to which it engenders a dialogue between new and old, encouraging students to digest what they do not yet know (the new information and skills they must learn) in terms of the familiar—their unofficial worlds, experience, and values. Certain kinds and features of classroom talk and writing assignments (e.g., discussion, authentic questions, journals, drafts, "learning logs," as we shall see in Chapter 4) afford far more opportunity and flexibility than others (e.g., most exams and essays used for examining purposes) for students to contextualize and assimilate new information. These particular kinds of instructional discourse are therefore potentially engaging.

In short, how students think—indeed the extent to which they really need to think in school—and consequently what they can learn depend a lot on how their teachers respond to their students' responses. This is the most fundamental way that classroom discourse shapes student learning: Specific modes or genres of discourse engender particular epistemic roles for the conversants, and these roles, in turn, engender, constrain, and empower their thinking. The bottom line for instruction is that the quality of student learning is closely linked to the quality of classroom talk. If we are to understand the structure of discourse in our classrooms and its relationship to our students' learning, then, we must look closely at the interactions and exchanges that constitute what Cazden (1988) calls "the language of learning." The insights we gain will enhance the learning potential of our instruction. The following chapters examine these ideas in empirical terms, focusing on the role of classroom and school discourse in student learning by contrasting the respective effects of monologically and dialogically organized instruction on learning.

CHAPTER 2

The Big Picture: Language and Learning in Hundreds of English Lessons

Martin Nystrand and Adam Gamoran

FEW GOOD MODELS currently exist for understanding how social processes affect student learning in classroom settings. There is widespread consensus that research must focus on teacher–student and peer interaction as it affects learning in order to be sensitive to the social context of learning. Yet most conceptions of instruction view learning as the result of what teachers plan and provide for students, that is, what teachers do to students. Adherents of this approach see instruction as a one-way transmission of knowledge from teacher and texts to students, and they typically assess students' knowledge for its congruence with curricular aims and objectives.

In our research in secondary school English classes, however, we had in mind not what teachers "do to students" but rather what teachers and their students do together, that is, what Michaels (1987) calls "the day-to-day practice of a 'curriculum'" (p. 323). In this sense, teacher and students negotiate the actual curriculum — as opposed to the ideal or intended curriculum (for example, as written up in a curriculum guide). Superficially, this negotiation is visible in the give-and-take of classroom talk (Flanders, 1970). However, such ostensible interaction clearly is pedagogically less significant than the cognitive interaction that occurs — or does not occur, as the case may be — between teacher and students. When minds meet in this way, the result is a sequence of shared understandings of subject matter among members of the class, and the course of instruction, whether considered on any given day or examined over an entire school year, may be analyzed in terms of how classroom talk and activities modify and expand these understandings. In this sense, dialogic instruction is a negotiation of meaning by and between teacher and students.

We observed hundreds of eighth- and ninth-grade lessons over 2 years. In all our observations, we never found the "perfectly dialogic classroom"; indeed, such a perfect classroom probably does not exist in the real world. Rather, we did a large empirical study to examine the general effects of dialogic practices on achievement and learning. The scope of our study, undertaken with a large sample of students in a large and diverse sample of classes, schools, and communities, enabled us to systematically test hypotheses about such practices.

This chapter reports details and findings from this study, sketching an overall portrait of classroom discourse in middle and high school English classes, and helping us address several important questions about classroom talk and student learning.

- What is instructional discourse generally like in eighth- and ninth-grade English and language arts classes?
- How much instruction is recitation? How much consists of discussion and small-group work?
- How much instruction is organized dialogically? Monologically?
- How does classroom discourse vary from middle to high school? By ability group? By subject? Among urban, suburban, and rural schools?
- How do these practices affect student learning about literature? Which interactions are appropriate and productive?

Our study, which shows the role that large-scale data analysis can play in the investigation of classroom interaction and its effects on learning, found that generally students learn more in classrooms organized more dialogically than monologically. For an overview of the entire study, see Figure 2.1.

STUDYING CLASSROOM DISCOURSE: DESIGN AND METHODS

In order to develop as comprehensive an understanding of classroom discourse as possible, our study coordinated three separate but related investigations:

1. *Surveys and interviews.* We sought first to determine practices and attitudes toward classroom discourse by surveying both students and teachers on various classroom practices; in addition, we interviewed the teachers to learn about their instructional methods and the context of instruction.
2. *Class observations.* Through direct observation, we investigated teachers' allocation of class time to various types of classroom discourse, including recitation, discussion, and small-group work. We collected data allowing us to gauge the quality of teacher–student interaction by focusing on the characteristics of questions asked by both teachers and students.
3. *Hypothesis testing.* Using statistical techniques, we examined the general effects of classroom practices and the organization of instruction on student achievement.

Figure 2.1A. Synopsis of Study—Design

The purpose of our research was to investigate the effects of instructional organization on student learning, contrasting the epistemologies of recitation and
discussion. This work was conducted in a 2-year study (1987–1989) in 16 middle and junior high schools and 9 high schools in eight midwestern urban, suburban, and rural communities. Participating were 58 eighth-grade and 54 ninth-
grade language arts and English classes, involving more than 1,100 students
each year. Each class was observed four times, twice in the fall and twice in the
spring, providing observational data for more than 200 lessons each year.

TRACKING

The study encompassed both middle and high school, following a subset of students as they moved into high school, in order to understand the mechanism and
effects of placement and tracking in high school. The study was designed to
provide systematic contrasts of instruction and learning in high- and low-track
classes.

INSTRUCTIONAL DISCOURSE

Instructional discourse was studied in two ways. First, observers timed instructional activities in order to determine the allocation of class time to various
activities, for example, question–answer, discussion, small-group work, seatwork, and other activities. In addition, observers recorded and coded both
teacher and student questions for dimensions of dialogic instruction, including
(1) *authenticity* (whether or not questions had "prespecified" answers), (2)
uptake (incorporation of previous answers into subsequent questions), and (3)
level of evaluation (extent to which the teacher allowed a student response to
modify the topic of discourse). More than 23,000 questions were coded. The
observational data were supplemented by teacher and student survey data and
end-of-year teacher interviews.

LEARNING

Learning about literature was tested with a written examination in the spring
based on several works of literature studied during the year. The test involved a
set of increasingly more probing questions, ranging from naming and/or
describing as many characters from each story as the student could remember,
and explaining the ending of each story to briefly explaining the themes and
conflicts of each story and relating theme, conflict, and ending. All students
answered the same general questions, although the details of the tests varied
depending on the titles studied and selected. For the ninth-grade test, students
wrote a brief essay on some character from their readings whom they admired,
and explained their admiration.

Figure 2.1B. Synopsis of Study—Results

OVERALL

Classroom discourse was overwhelmingly monologic. When teachers were not lecturing, students mainly were either answering questions or completing seatwork. The teacher asked nearly all the questions, few questions were authentic, and few teachers followed up student responses. On average, discussion lasted less than 50 seconds per class in eighth grade and less than 15 seconds per class in ninth grade. Small-group work in eighth grade took only about half a minute each day, and only a little more than 2 minutes a day in grade 9.

PROCEDURAL VARIABLES

The study found a modest effect for time spent on homework, no effect for asking questions in class, and a negative effect for level of activity during recitation.

DIALOGIC INSTRUCTION

Results provided support for dialogic instruction, indicating that time devoted to discussion, authentic questions, uptake, and high-level teacher evaluation had a strong positive effect on achievement. Discussion in grade 8 had a particularly large effect.

IMPORTANCE OF CONTENT

Results of the grade 9 study were consistent with grade 8 results but only when controlled for content. Discussion and authentic questions unrelated to literature had a negative effect on learning.

GROUPWORK

Groupwork was successful to the extent that teachers clearly defined goals and tasks at the same time that they encouraged students to generate conclusions, solve open-ended problems, and address authentic questions rather than simply manipulate information and answer study questions. Most small-group work in study classes was in fact "collaborative seatwork," however, which had a negative effect on learning.

TRACKING

Instruction was more fragmented, contrived, and monologic in low-track than in high-track classes. In grade 8, teachers lectured 40% more in low-track classes than in high-track ones, and low-track discussion time was only half that of high-track groups. In grade 9, seatwork was nearly four times more frequent in low-track than in high-track classes.

Table 2.1. Characteristics of School Sample

	Number of Schools		
School District Type	Total	Middle Schools	High Schools
Parochial	8	6	2
Public	17	10	7
Small town/rural	6	3	3
Suburban	3	2	1
Urban	8	5	3

Research Sites and Participants

Our study lasted 2 years: Eighth-grade classes were observed during 1987–88, ninth-grade classes during 1988–89. We collected data in eight midwestern communities, including rural, urban, and suburban sites, in both public and parochial schools. Six of these communities were public school districts; the other two were Catholic high schools with students from a number of urban and suburban K–8 feeder schools. Unlike ninth-grade classes, which were all called English, eighth-grade classes were variously called language arts, English, reading, communications, literature, and so on; we selected the eighth-grade classes that focused most on reading. Table 2.1 provides a breakdown of the community and school types that participated in our study.

In each school we observed four English classes. In the smaller schools, we observed all the English classes; in the larger schools, we selected a representative sample of different ability groups as defined by the school (honors or accelerated, regular or average, basic or remedial). In all we made 451 observations in 58 eighth-grade classes in 16 middle and junior high schools, and 54 ninth-grade classes in nine high schools (which were fed by the junior high and middle schools in our eighth-grade study). Between 1,100 and 1,200 students participated each year; of all eligible students, about 10% were lost through absence or refusal. About one-third of all students participated in both years of the study. Table 2.2 summarizes these data.

Observational Procedures

Each class was visited four times by a trained observer, twice during fall semester and twice during spring semester.[1] Within these parameters, observations were scheduled at the mutual convenience of teachers and observers. On these occasions, the observer noted the time spent in different instructional activities, and recorded and coded all teacher and student questions for a set of variables contrasting monologic and dialogic instruction (coding is explained on pp. 37f.).

Table 2.2. Scope of Study

Characteristics	Grade 8	Grade 9
Number of students	1,041	1,100
Number of classes	58	54
Number of times each class observed	4	4
Number of observations	227	224
Number of coded questions	12,033	11,043

Discourse Episodes and Segments

Data from each class session were organized according to episodes and segments. An *episode* was defined as a coherent classroom activity centering around a particular objective or purpose. A new episode was marked when the teacher addressed a new objective. Like the start of a new paragraph, each such shift usually was evident in the teacher's initiation of a new topic. Usually episodes consisted of two or more activities. For example, in addressing a particular objective, a teacher might initiate a question-and-answer session that then would be interrupted by brief periodic lectures and culminate in a homework assignment. When something like this happened, we divided the episode into *segments,* defined as any coherent part of an episode that differed from other activities of the episode. Instructional activities were classified with durations in minutes and seconds for the following:

1. *Classroom management activities*
   Classroom procedures
   Directions
   Discipline
2. *Direct instruction*
   Lecture, film
   Question-answer
   Discussion
   Student presentations
   Students reading aloud
3. *Seatwork*
   Supervised with teacher helping
   Supervised with teacher monitoring
   Unsupervised
   Small-group work
4. *Tests and quizzes*

When the teacher did one thing (e.g., lecture) and some students were allowed to do another (e.g., when the teacher lectured to part of the class but individualized instruction for others by assigning them seatwork), or the teacher did not object to some doing work unrelated to the lecture, we classified the activity that most students did. Observers wrote a brief description of each episode and recorded and coded each question asked by either the teacher or students.

We defined discussion as the free exchange of information among students and/or between at least three students and the teacher that lasted at least a half minute. Typically discussions came about during question–answer exchanges when a student would volunteer an observation (rather than ask a question) that the teacher allowed to substitute for normal evaluation. These discussions, which interrupted or violated the normal initiation-response-evaluation (IRE) sequence of recitation, included few questions, and those that were asked typically clarified ideas and information ("By that do you mean . . . ?").

Questions

Bakhtin's conception of discourse encompasses far more than just questions and the utterances immediately preceding and following them: As we saw in Chapter 1, Bakhtin's chains of utterances also encompass frames of mind and core beliefs, including those related to students' experience out of school. Dialogic analysis is most directly accomplished through close analysis of transcripts of individual lessons and other forms of qualitative analysis, especially of the sort Dyson undertakes in her *Social Worlds of Children Learning to Write* (1993). Although our study undertook some such analysis (see Chapter 3), the main focus of our research was a comprehensive analysis of classroom discourse, generally with a special focus on teacher and student questions. We did this for several reasons. First, we wanted to capture the general dimensions of instruction, requiring us to examine hundreds of instructional episodes and lessons. We focused on question–answer exchanges because they provide an effective method for such a general analysis, and because they are so central to instruction, occupying 30% of class time in the eighth-grade classes we studied and 42% in the ninth-grade classes. Question–answer exchanges between teachers and students clearly dominate instruction for most students. They play a key role in both accommodating and excluding student voices in the public, authoritative discourse of the classroom, and they are the central instructional mechanism in American classrooms for assigning epistemic roles to students. As such, they significantly regulate the extent to which teacher–student interaction can be dialogic.

Two features of questions were of particular interest to us: *authenticity* (whether or not teacher questions had "prespecified" answers) and *uptake* (incorporation of previous answers into subsequent questions). Each is a critical variable affecting the salience of student voices in classroom discourse, and reflecting how far the horizons of classroom discourse extend beyond the question–answer sequences themselves to draw on student experience central to student engagement. While these data cannot detail the dynamics of particular teacher–student interactions, they nonetheless provide a powerful index of the extent to which teachers open their classes to student voices when they ask the questions they do.

Questions are not everything, of course, and authentic questions, we found, do not invariably produce learning. Nonetheless, one must not underestimate the role teachers' questions play in shaping the character of classroom discourse as it affects learning. Questions presume answers. As negotiations of sorts, question–answer sequences reveal important features of teacher–student interaction and hence the character of instruction. Much can be learned about teacher–student interaction and talk in a classroom by determining the source of questions, the extent of authenticity and uptake, the level of cognitive activity that questions elicit, and so on. Even the pace of a teacher's questioning can be revealing: Carlsen (1991) cites studies finding that a slow pace of teacher questioning and extended wait times correlate with greater numbers of student responses (Honea, 1982), as well as more sustained student responses of greater complexity and higher-order thinking (Fagan, Hassler, & Szabl, 1981).

Early in our study, we learned that the vast proportion of teacher questions (a) are test questions, (b) get a response, (c) do not involve uptake, and (d) elicit a report of what is already known. Indeed, this is the very profile of monologic classroom discourse, and we soon began to describe such questions, unfortunately, as normal teacher questions. The following questions, all from Mr. Schmidt's lesson described in Chapter 1, are examples:

- "According to the poet, what is the subject of *The Iliad?*"
- "Where does the action of the first part of Book I take place when we enter the story?"
- "What is the result of the quarrel between Agamemnon and Achilles?"

We used data about questions to build profiles of instruction and classroom discourse, coding more than 23,000 questions, and examining each question in the context of the whole lesson at the time it was asked.[2] Ninth-grade classes were tape recorded. Whenever observers were uncertain about how to interpret classroom activities and code questions, they consulted with the teacher after class. Questions were coded for

- *Source:* Teacher or student
- *Response:* Yes or no
- *Authenticity:* Whether or not an answer was prespecified
- *Uptake:* Incorporation of a previous answer into a subsequent question

- *Cognitive level:* The type of cognitive demand made by the question
- *Level of evaluation:* Whether the teacher valorized and elaborated the students' responses

Coding reliabilities were based on paired readings of a sample of questions.[3]

During the ninth-grade study, observers collected data using a specially written computer program, CLASS 2.0,[4] during class. This program helped with question coding, as well as the allocation and timing of various instructional activities, which the observer recorded by selecting from a menu and then briefly described. Every 5 minutes during question–answer exchanges and every 2 minutes during seatwork and lecture, the program prompted the observer to record the number of students obviously off task,[5] as well as the number actively participating, and to make adjustments in the number of students in case any recently had entered or left the classroom.

During question–answer exchanges, the observer typed in and coded the questions that teachers and students asked during instruction. As observers entered each question into computer memory, the program prompted them for codings. When data collection was completed, CLASS-EDIT 2.0, a companion program to CLASS 2.0, allowed proofreading, editing, and revising of each file for inappropriate codings, and then computed basic statistics for each episode. Generally, we were satisfied that these procedures were minimally intrusive to instruction during our observations.

Authenticity. Authentic questions are questions for which the asker has not prespecified an answer and include requests for information as well as open-ended questions with indeterminate answers. Dialogically, authentic teacher questions signal to students the teacher's interest in what they think and know and not just whether they can report what someone else thinks or has said. Authentic questions invite students to contribute something new to the discussion that can change or modify it in some way.

By contrast, a *test question* allows students no control over the flow of the discussion. Because authentic questions allow an indeterminate number of acceptable answers and open the floor to students' ideas, they work dialogically. By contrast, a test question allows only one possible right answer, and is hence monologic (in Lotman's terms, univocal; see Chapter 1).

Before we started our observations, we worried that determining the authenticity of questions might be complicated and unreliable since such determination requires assessing teachers' intentions; authenticity cannot be determined from words alone. For example, "Who won the World Series in 1928?" can be either a test question or an authentic question depending on (a) whether the asker knows the answer and wants to see if the person asked also knows, in which case it is a test question, or (b) whether the asker doesn't know and wants to find out by asking someone who does know, in which case it is authentic.

The nature of the activity, that is, the genre of classroom discourse, we discovered, is the most reliable indicator of authenticity. Hence, when teachers began a lesson by saying, "Okay, class, let's check the answers to your study questions," we quickly learned that the questions were invariably test questions (although follow-up discussions of students' answers were sometimes authentic). By contrast, when teachers asked about students' personal experiences as lead-ins, for example, to open-ended discussions of a poem or short story, we found that these questions were authentic. In Chapter 1, Ms. Turner's initial question, "Can you recall things from *Huck Finn* that, um, seemed racist to you?" is an example. Questions asked during discussions, for example, the question Tom asks John in Ms. Lindsay's class, "Is it Mr. Hollings's store? Is that it?" are also authentic since their purpose is not testing someone's knowledge but rather exchanging only that information the person asking the question actually needed to know.

Whenever the authenticity of a question was unclear or ambiguous to us, we consulted the teacher. In practice (and somewhat to our initial surprise), coding authenticity proved to be generally quite straightforward. We quickly learned that most classroom discourse is not subtle: The vast proportion of questions teachers ask are test questions, whereas student questions are virtually always authentic (except when students role play teachers; then they ask test questions!).

Uptake. Uptake occurs when one conversant, for example, a teacher, asks someone else, for example, a student, about something the other person said previously (Collins, 1982). Here is an example of uptake from a ninth-grade lesson on *The Iliad:* The teacher asks, "What do they have to do to Polyphemus?" A student replies, "Blind him." The teacher then follows up, asking, "How come the plan is for blinding Cyclops?" Uptake occurs here when the teacher picks up on the student's response, asking about "blinding" him. Uptake often is marked by the use of pronouns, for example, "How did *it* work?"; "What caused *it*?"; "What city grew out of *this*?" In each of these questions, the italicized pronoun refers to a previous answer.[6] Uptake also may be characterized by ellipsis. In Ms. Turner's class, for example, when Linda says that racism in *The Adventures of Huckleberry Finn* makes her "ashamed," Ms. Turner's reply, "In what way?" exhibits uptake since her question makes Linda's answer the momentary topic of discourse.[7] Teachers use uptake whenever they follow up on student responses. As an essential dialogic resource facilitating the negotiation of understandings, uptake plays a prominent role in discussion as conversants listen and respond appropriately to each other.

Cognitive Level. Our project also sought to assess whether the cognitive level of questioning affects student learning. In this way we examined whether instruction stressing higher-order thinking is necessarily dialogic. We therefore coded the level of cognitive functioning that each question sought to elicit, judging it high to the extent that the question could not be answered "through the routine application of previously learned knowledge" (Newmann, 1990, p. 44; see also Polanyi's (1958) distinction between routine performances and heuristic acts). Like authenticity, the cognitive level of questions cannot be judged altogether from words alone. For example, if the teacher expected students to answer questions by reciting information found in textbooks, we coded questions as reports regardless of their linguistic structure. Hence, although a why-question normally will elicit an analysis, it will elicit a report if the teacher's focus is the recitation of a textbook's analysis rather than the class' reflection; then "Why?" really means, "According to your text, why did it happen this way? Do you remember?" Factors affecting the cognitive level of any question include the following:

1. *Source of the question.* The same question that elicits an analysis from a person who has to figure things out may well elicit a report from another, more knowledgeable individual who already knows and simply needs to explain. For example, "Why did Odysseus and his men plan deliberately to blind Polyphemus?" may elicit an analysis from students (assuming, of course, that they have to figure out the answer and not merely recite their textbook on the point), but most likely will elicit a report if a *student* asks a *teacher* who already knows the answer. When we were unclear, we asked about it after class.
2. *Experience, ability, and prior knowledge* of the person answering the question, whether student or teacher. If student answers seemed to require routine cognitive operation, we coded questions as eliciting reports. We defined prior knowledge as "prior to the previous night's homework."[8]
3. *Nature of the instructional activity.* When an episode was devoted to review, our normal expectation for responses was a report, even if questions had the linguistic form of higher-level questions (e.g., "What's the difference between a symbol and an image?" when asked as a study question).
4. *Source of information* required by the question. Information sources include prior experience, textbooks, and previous teacher lectures.

Level of cognition elicited by questions was measured on a five-point linear scale calibrated for level of abstraction and derived from Applebee (1981), Britton, Burgess, Martin, McLeod, and Rosen (1975), and Moffett (1968). Levels were as follows:

1   *Record* of an ongoing event: What's happening?
2   *Recitation and report* of old information: What happened?

3 *Generalization:* What happens?
4 *Analysis:* Why does it happen?
5 *Speculation:* What might happen?

We coded questions as records if they elicited descriptions of what students were observing, feeling, or thinking at the time of the question. Examples include: "Any questions on that?" and "What [or why] are you thinking about that?" If the question required students to think and not just report something already known or previously thought by someone else, then we scored cognitive level higher than 2. Determining the level involved judging whether the student answering the question was building up a generalization, in which case we scored it a 3, or breaking down an argument, in which case we coded it as an analysis and rated its cognitive level as 4. Generalizations display inductive reasoning, building up ideas rather than breaking them down. They address questions such as: "What happens?" and "What do I make of what happens?" They tie things together; they are not restatements of information. Analyses display deductive reasoning, breaking concepts, ideas, and arguments down rather than building up ideas. To be scored as analyses, questions had to require more than restatements of known information. Questions were judged to be lower order (i.e., eliciting records or reports) if they elicited old information, or higher order (i.e., eliciting generalizations, analyses, or speculations) if they elicited new information and could not be answered through the routine application of prior knowledge.[9]

Unless texts explicitly stated the answers to teachers' questions, we judged most questions about literary texts to be either generalizations or analyses. Hence, from a ninth-grade class session on *To Kill a Mockingbird*, the question, "How does Tom die?" elicited a report since the answer is stated in the novel. By contrast, "What's the overall reaction of most of Maycomb's citizens?" elicited an analysis since the answer required taking into account and relating disparate information from the text. We found that questions like, "What is the meaning of *x*?" or "What is *x*?" elicited either (a) a *report* if, in recitation, the teacher's intent was to see whether students knew it; (b) a *generalization* if *x* was a word and the teacher's intent was to elicit an original definition; or (c) an *analysis* if *x* was a phrase in a book, a line in a play, a symbol, and so forth, and the teacher asked students to situate or relate a part of the text (phrase, line, symbol) to the whole, for example, "So how do we explain *x*?" In these cases we coded recitations of meaning as reports, and explications of meaning as generalizations and analyses.

THE PREVALENCE OF MONOLOGIC INSTRUCTION

The results of our research found most classroom discourse to be overwhelmingly monologic. In this regard, our study replicates numerous previous studies documenting the historical and widespread prevalence of recitation in American schools. Indeed, as early as 1860, Morrison complained that "young teachers are very apt to confound rapid questioning and answers with sure and effective teaching" (cited in Hoetker & Ahlbrand, 1969, p. 153). In 1912, Stevens complained that the widespread practice of recitation made "the classroom the place for displaying knowledge instead of a laboratory for getting and using it" (p. 16). In 1919, Colvin estimated that only "about five percent [of the teacher questions he studied] could be considered in any way genuine thought questions" (p. 269). Writing about the same time, Miller (1922) complained that teachers were unable to "endure the silence that must prevail while the pupil is thinking and organizing his material" (quoted in Hoetker & Ahlbrand, 1969, p. 154). Thayer (1928) claimed that recitation was a progressive reform enabling teachers to gauge the mastery of large groups of children by checking the knowledgeability of relatively few. Corey (1940), Bellack, Kliebard, Hyman, and Smith (1966), and Hoetker (1967) all found that teachers talked about two-thirds of all instructional time and that more than 80% of all teacher questions sought to elicit recall in a recitation format. Recent studies continue to find similar results; see Duffy (1981), Durkin (1978–79), Hoetker and Ahlbrand (1969), Goodlad (1984), Sarason (1983), and Tharp and Gallimore (1988).

Class Time

Our study generally replicates these depressingly enduring findings. Recitation and lecture were common. When teachers were not lecturing, students mainly were either answering questions or engaged in seatwork. Indeed, on average, 85% of each class day in both eighth- and ninth-grade classes was devoted to a combination of lecture, question-and-answer recitation, and seatwork. Discussion and small-group work were rare. On average, discussion took 50 seconds per class in eighth grade and less than 15 seconds in grade 9;[10] small-group work, which occupied about half a minute a day in eighth grade, took a bit more than 2 minutes a day in grade 9.[11]

In grade 8, more than two-thirds of all classes had at least 10 minutes of seatwork daily, and 31% had 20 minutes or more daily; only one class had no seatwork at all. Half of all classes had at least 10 minutes a day of question-and-answer activity, and 17.2% had 20 minutes or more. All but two classes routinely involved lecture; teachers in four of the 58 classes lectured 21 minutes or more each day. Overall means for all eighth-grade class activities are summarized in Table 2.3.

In ninth grade, time spent on lecture increased from 5 to 8 minutes per day (26% of all class time), and question–answer recitation increased from 12 to almost 18 minutes per day. Lecture was so ubiquitous that less than 2% of

Table 2.3. Grade 8 Allocation of Instructional Time to Various Activities (mean minutes per class day)

	All Classes		Low-Track Classes		High-Track Classes		Urban Classes		Suburban Classes		Rural Classes	
Lecture	5.33	(7.23)	3.84	(2.91)	2.31	(1.94)	6.43	(9.19)	4.02	(2.77)	4.82	(3.28)
Question-Answer	12.27	(6.76)	13.06	(6.48)	12.12	(7.75)	9.46	(5.97)	14.47	(5.78)	18.56	(5.60)
Discussion	0.86	(1.79)	0.84	(1.98)	1.97	(2.68)	0.75	(1.49)	0.84	(1.88)	1.69	(3.38)
Student presentations	0.36	(1.46)	0.00	(0.00)	0.77	(2.62)	0.30	(1.65)	0.58	(1.34)	0.03	(0.08)
Students reading aloud	2.76	(4.79)	3.83	(4.74)	2.52	(3.36)	3.11	(5.83)	2.48	(3.20)	2.46	(2.04)
Seatwork												
Teacher helping	1.86	(4.76)	4.23	(8.34)	0.33	(0.55)	1.70	(2.87)	2.70	(7.44)	0.06	(0.19)
Supervised	15.18	(12.15)	11.67	(9.12)	15.44	(13.30)	18.71	(14.04)	11.15	(7.09)	8.58	(5.78)
Unsupervised	0.61	(3.51)	0.17	(0.58)	2.11	(7.38)	0.99	(4.63)	0.13	(0.41)	0.09	(0.19)
Tests and quizzes	1.11	(2.35)	0.84	(3.27)	1.94	(3.07)	1.10	(2.76)	1.31	(1.92)	1.14	(1.98)
Small-group work	0.65	(2.50)	0.00	(0.00)	1.63	(3.94)	0.55	(2.45)	1.03	(2.95)	0.00	(0.00)
	$N = 58$		$N = 15$		$N = 13$		$N = 39$		$N = 8$		$N = 11$	

Notes: Statistics in parentheses are standard deviations. Times given for tests and quizzes are underestimated because we tried not to schedule observations on days when they were given.

all classes had none at all, and half the classes heard 8 minutes or more of lecture daily (one class actually had an average of more than 27 minutes a day). All classes involved question-and-answer recitation; 50% had at least 16 minutes daily (two classes averaged more than 30 minutes of recitation each day). Only two classes had no seatwork at all; at least 10 minutes daily was common for nearly a third of all classes. Overall, results on use of class time document the clearly monologic character of classroom discourse in the classes we observed. Overall means for use of class time in grade 9 are summarized in Table 2.4.

Questions

The character of instructional questions in the classes we observed was consistent with the monologic organization of class time. More commonly than not, students were treated as "empty vessels" to be "filled" by teachers. In virtually all classes, the teacher asked nearly all the questions; few about literature were authentic, and equally few followed up on student responses. In the eighth-grade classes (see Table 2.5), about 35 questions on average were asked during each class, 92% of them by the teacher. Only 12% of the teacher questions were authentic, and only 11% exhibited uptake.[12] In the ninth-grade classes (see Table 2.6), teachers asked more than 52 questions each class period on average, or about 50% more than in the eighth-grade classes: 54% of all questions involved recitation. These results help explain National Assessment of Education Progress (NAEP) results, which perennially show that American students are far more proficient at literal comprehension than at analysis and critical thinking (see, e.g., Applebee, Langer, Mullis, Latham, & Gentile, 1994).

Given the infrequency of authentic questions in eighth grade, we were surprised to find that the proportion in ninth-grade classes was twice as high. Indeed, authentic questions were asked in all the ninth-grade classes we observed; half the classes routinely had 25% or more. In subsequent analysis, we discovered that much of the increase was due to the use of authentic questions to inquire about nonacademic topics. Uptake also was more common in ninth-grade classes, exhibited by 26% of all questions.[13] Like eighth-grade instruction, however, most ninth-grade classroom interaction tended to be monologic, permitting little opportunity for substantive exchange.

Track Differences

The near-universal preference for "recitable information" afflicted low-track classes even more than regular- and high-track classes since low-track classes typically got a refracted, watered down, fragmented rendition of the

Table 2.4. Grade 9 Allocation of Instructional Time to Various Activities (mean minutes per class day)

	All Classes		Low-Track Classes		High-Track Classes		Urban Classes		Suburban Classes		Rural Classes	
Lecture	8.42	(5.84)	8.58	(4.86)	9.04	(8.46)	8.53	(6.21)	7.46	(7.58)	8.58	(2.98)
Question-Answer	17.58	(6.55)	15.62	(4.27)	22.17	(6.45)	18.11	(5.65)	15.23	(6.45)	17.57	(9.18)
Discussion	0.24	(0.50)	0.31	(0.51)	0.37	(0.75)	0.29	(0.56)	0.00	(0.00)	0.28	(0.47)
Student presentations	1.44	(2.69)	0.32	(0.49)	1.59	(3.33)	1.50	(2.32)	2.92	(4.84)	0.19	(0.42)
Students reading aloud	2.38	(3.15)	4.87	(4.96)	0.81	(1.36)	2.33	(3.05)	0.72	(1.33)	3.75	(3.93)
Seatwork												
Teacher helping	1.99	(3.05)	2.97	(3.81)	0.92	(1.78)	1.69	(3.05)	1.29	(2.07)	3.47	(3.41)
Supervised	6.23	(5.54)	9.77	(6.13)	2.52	(2.11)	5.70	(5.39)	6.60	(6.34)	7.67	(5.68)
Unsupervised	0.11	(0.36)	0.03	(0.10)	0.07	(0.15)	0.05	(0.11)	0.04	(0.11)	0.35	(0.76)
Tests and quizzes	1.28	(1.99)	0.55	(0.84)	1.40	(1.95)	1.29	(2.14)	2.76	(1.75)	0.15	(0.39)
Small-group work	2.25	(4.44)	1.00	(2.71)	2.71	(5.26)	2.19	(4.51)	4.41	(6.24)	0.88	(1.39)
	$N = 54$		$N = 9$		$N = 13$		$N = 35$		$N = 8$		$N = 11$	

Notes: Statistics in parentheses are standard deviations. Times given for tests and quizzes are underestimated because we tried not to schedule observations on days when they were given.

Table 2.5. Properties of Classroom Questions in Grade 8 Literature Classes

| Class Type | Average Number of Questions per Class Session | Proportion of | | | | | | Mean Cognitive Level | Proportion of Students Off Task | Average Class Size |
		Asked by Teacher	Uptake	Authentic Teacher Questions	No Response	High-Level Evaluation	High-Level Cognition			
All classes	34.62 (17.37)	0.92 (0.16)	0.11 (0.07)	0.10 (0.11)	0.02 (0.03)	0.03 (0.04)	0.36 (0.15)	2.66 (0.29)	0.05 (0.06)	20.66 (7.31)
Low track	36.91 (18.71)	0.97 (0.05)	0.11 (0.08)	0.12 (0.12)	0.04 (0.04)	0.02 (0.04)	0.37 (0.12)	2.69 (0.29)	0.08 (0.10)	18.80 (7.72)
High track	41.97 (20.91)	0.93 (0.09)	0.16 (0.07)	0.12 (0.10)	0.02 (0.03)	0.03 (0.04)	0.40 (0.14)	2.76 (0.27)	0.02 (0.02)	21.08 (7.89)
Urban	29.22 (18.25)	0.89 (0.20)	0.10 (0.06)	0.13 (0.10)	0.03 (0.03)	0.04 (0.05)	0.36 (0.15)	2.68 (0.30)	0.06 (0.08)	21.91 (7.63)
Suburban	42.52 (14.99)	0.96 (0.04)	0.14 (0.07)	0.12 (0.14)	0.01 (0.02)	0.02 (0.03)	0.40 (0.14)	2.70 (0.26)	0.02 (0.03)	20.00 (6.86)
Rural	41.11 (9.22)	0.98 (0.02)	0.11 (0.08)	0.06 (0.05)	0.04 (0.04)	0.02 (0.03)	0.25 (0.12)	2.46 (0.20)	0.04 (0.04)	19.00 (6.58)

Notes: N = 58 classes, including 15 low-track and 13 high-track classes, and 39 urban, 8 suburban, and 11 rural classes. Numbers in parentheses are standard deviations.

Table 2.6. Properties of Classroom Questions in Grade 9 Literature Classes

| Class Type | Average Number of Questions per Class Session | Proportion of | | | | | | Mean Cognitive Level | Proportion of Students Off Task | Average Class Size |
		Asked by Teacher	Uptake	Authentic Teacher Questions	No Response	High-Level Evaluation	High-Level Cognition			
All classes	52.77 (20.25)	0.91 (0.10)	0.26 (0.12)	0.27 (0.19)	0.03 (0.03)	0.01 (0.02)	0.46 (0.19)	2.91 (0.38)	0.04 (0.04)	22.74 (6.36)
Low track	48.62 (22.35)	0.94 (0.05)	0.27 (0.13)	0.25 (0.19)	0.03 (0.04)	0.01 (0.02)	0.47 (0.14)	2.95 (0.35)	0.05 (0.04)	15.00 (4.27)
High track	60.05 (11.61)	0.89 (0.12)	0.26 (0.11)	0.28 (0.18)	0.03 (0.02)	0.01 (0.01)	0.44 (0.21)	2.85 (0.37)	0.02 (0.03)	25.38 (5.75)
Urban	53.78 (20.80)	0.92 (0.09)	0.27 (0.13)	0.33 (0.19)	0.03 (0.04)	0.02 (0.03)	0.52 (0.23)	2.99 (0.41)	0.04 (0.05)	24.63 (6.63)
Suburban	45.50 (15.28)	0.82 (0.16)	0.24 (0.12)	0.22 (0.16)	0.02 (0.01)	0.00 (0.00)	0.26 (0.14)	2.51 (0.28)	0.05 (0.04)	21.88 (3.23)
Rural	54.83 (22.12)	0.96 (0.04)	0.22 (0.10)	0.09 (0.04)	0.02 (0.02)	0.00 (0.01)	0.45 (0.20)	2.89 (0.40)	0.03 (0.02)	18.80 (5.19)

Notes: $N = 54$ classes, including 9 low-track and 13 high-track classes, and 35 urban, 8 suburban, and 11 rural classes. Numbers in parentheses are standard deviations.

regular curriculum; it was as if low-track students were to understand a book by dealing only with the index (Page, 1991). Our data also show that low-track students, in contrast to high-track students, engaged in far more clerical as opposed to compositional tasks; indeed many of their so-called "writing" tasks, such as filling-in-the-blanks, were not discourse at all. Their writing was more formulaic, and the level of response to their writing was low. In these low-track classes, the terms of reciprocity were limited mainly to procedures.

To examine differences between high- and low-track classes, we compared the two groups on allocation of instructional time and all discourse variables. In eighth grade, both groups spent 40% or more class time doing seatwork. The biggest differences were in time devoted to lecture — the teacher lectured to low-track students 40% more than to high-track students — and to discussion, which occupied nearly twice as much time in high-track classes than in low, hence giving a more dialogic tone to the high-track classes (even though the proportion of authentic teacher questions and uptake did not differ much). In ninth grade, seatwork occupied almost 13 minutes a day (29% of instructional time) in the low-track classes but less than 4 minutes (8%) in the high-track classes. Both groups spent close to 9 minutes in lecture and less than 1 minute in discussion, but the high-track classes spent more time doing small-group work and answering questions. (Tables 2.3 and 2.5 show some of these results for grade 8; Tables 2.4 and 2.6 provide a breakdown for grade 9.)

These results are consistent with our earlier research (Nystrand & Gamoran, 1988), which found that students in low-achieving classes are far more likely than their higher-achieving counterparts to be involved in fragmented, contrived learning. Using survey data, we found that students in low-achieving eighth- and ninth-grade English classes

- Did grammar exercises 2.6 times as frequently as did their high-achieving counterparts
- Did reports 2.4 times as frequently
- Filled in blanks 5 times as often
- Answered true–false questions 4 times as frequently
- Completed multiple-choice questions 4.1 times as often

In their responses to the papers of students in low-achieving classes, teachers commented

- 2.3 times as much about spelling (in marginal and terminal comments)
- 1.8 times as much about punctuation
- 2 times as much about grammar

In their responses to high-achieving students' papers, however, teachers commented

- 1.7 and 1.9 times as much about content (in marginal and terminal comments, respectively) compared with teacher comments on low-track papers

Teachers held writing conferences with low-ability students about as infrequently (about once a month on average) as with high-achieving students. However, in these conferences they discussed spelling 2.6 times as much with students in low-achieving classes, and they discussed content 1.9 times as frequently with high-achieving students.

Why these differences? To answer this question, we looked closely at interviews of the teachers in our study and then compared what they said with what we observed in their classes. First, despite considerable lip service to "discussion," we observed little discussion in any classes in the sense of in-depth exchanges of ideas in the absence of teacher evaluation. Most teachers who spoke readily of their value for "discussion"—and indeed there were a great many—really enacted some version of recitation. Discussion almost always turned out to be what one teacher described as "question-and-answer discussion" involving a prescripted, teacher-set exchange. Such discussion was rarely collaborative, thoroughgoing, pushed-to-the-limit sharing and exploration of student ideas unfolding in class—what Britton (1970) described as a "struggle to organize . . . thoughts and feelings, to come up with words that . . . shape an understanding, [a] struggle to rise above the limitations of [the] language" (p. 12). What mainly varied in the lessons we observed was the length of students' responses as they answered teachers' questions.

Some other teachers expressed a conception of discussion best described as forensic. One teacher, who taught academically talented ninth-grade English in a large urban high school, believed that schooling too much favors docile, cooperative students; in contrast, he liked aggressively expressive, openly assertive students who could readily state and defend their points of view and were willing to argue in class, even with him. Right answers weren't enough in his classes, he said; students had to be able to support them and prevail. Needless to say, this conception of discussion as debate favored the most confident, verbally articulate, and competitive of students. This was a view most commonly heard in suburban schools and was expressed almost exclusively by male teachers (most of the suburban teachers in our study were male; most of the urban teachers were female).

Given these conceptions of discussion—one recitation, the other debate—it is perhaps not surprising that students tracked into low-ability classes proved hesitant or "reticent" in the classroom, as their teachers often described them. In observations, these students often seemed unsure of what teachers were looking for, and responded to teachers' questions with shy, cryptic guesses (marked by rising intonation patterns) more often than "answers" (as Mr. Schmidt's students did; see Chapter 1). In the homogeneously grouped classes, low-ability students readily stepped out of the way of the more confident students. Many of them, especially those with reading problems, did not do homework, and some became discipline problems in class.

When students did not complete reading assignments for homework, many teachers stopped assigning much and devoted substantial proportions of class time to reading aloud. They would pick very short (2–3 page) stories that could be both read aloud and followed up with either seatwork or "discussion," all in the confines of a 50-minute class period. One teacher told us she deliberately avoided open-ended questions with these students because she felt obligated to prepare them for standardized reading tests in the spring. She therefore concentrated on who, what, and when—though not so much on why—and very few of her questions focused on the special demands of literature (as opposed to nonfiction informative prose). Newspaper stories might have served just as well, and in fact did, especially in many urban classes. Needless to say, the discourse in these classes was heavily monologic, and students' recollections of these very short stories, to say nothing of their understanding, were ephemeral, as we learned when we gave our own test in the spring.

One eighth-grade English teacher at a junior high school in a small homogeneous midwestern town was typical of these teachers. She liked tracking because she felt it allowed her to give each of the groups the attention they needed. She previously had taught mixed-ability classes, and she said the slower students invariably "got lost" because they were "unable to compete with their college-bound peers"; as they became frustrated, moreover, they got into trouble. In her school, she said, the advanced students covered a lot more. This teacher described her idea of an ideal lesson as the engaged, authentic discussion of students expressing and defending their opinions and relating their readings to their personal experience, and she found this far easier to do with high-track than with low-track students. The high-track students were better readers, so she could reasonably assign more reading for homework; class time, then, was for discussion. The high-track class read four novels; the low-track class read two. The low-ability students needed a lot of help with reading, and they often did not complete assigned readings as homework. Hence, she devoted a lot of class time to "decoding" and reading aloud; this left little time for discussion. Moreover, the low-track students were far "more reticent" about expressing their opinions and "less adept" at relating their readings to their own experience than were their comparatively confident and "garrulous" high-ability classmates, so this made it far easier, she said, to engage the high-track students in discussion. She did not seem to realize that these differences in pedagogy and interaction afforded the two groups of students significantly different learning opportunities, especially favoring the high-ability students at the expense of the low (Gamoran, Nystrand, Berends, & LePore, 1995).

Far more teachers supported ability grouping than opposed it. Those opposing it were far more likely to be in suburban and rural schools than in urban schools, where opposition was very rare. Rural teachers, who seemed to view school as part of extended families in their small towns, were more concerned than the other teachers about possible negative effects on the learning and self-image of their slower students, who in tracked groups would not "have anyone to model or peers with good behavior and good skills," as one teacher put it. Several suburban teachers particularly were disaffected with high-ability students, whom one described as "pseudo-intellectuals and pseudo-sophisiticates" who tended to be "abrasive." Another teacher said, "Sometimes the higher-level kids get an attitude that 'I'm superior — I don't have to work hard.'" Some suburban teachers felt that mixed grouping could benefit average students. They thought it could improve student writing by expanding the stock of shared experience in the class: "Writing is based on experience," said one. Others thought it could stimulate discussion and improve literature instruction. Yet these teachers were in the minority. We interviewed only one teacher who claimed that while mixed-ability groups might make it more difficult to teach, they also made it "more fun." "They're more real," she claimed.

Most teachers, however, were content to teach tracked classes. Some candidly said they were better able to engage the high-ability students than the low simply because they had more in common with the high-ability students; they had more to talk about together. One such teacher taught eighth-grade reading to "basic" students and literature to "academically talented" students in a midwestern urban junior high. At her school, IQ scores played a major role in assigning students to different ability groups, and she agreed that her academically talented students were "innately brighter," especially able to manipulate multiple points of view, and more likely than her basic students to go beyond the literal meaning of their readings. She believed that mixing students of different abilities shortchanged everyone: If teachers pitched things toward the higher-ability students, she explained, they lost the slower students; if they made adjustments for the slower students, their classes were not as stimulating for the faster students. Hence, she felt such students needed to be separated from the basic students "for their own good." She preferred teaching the academically talented because she could do more things with them — "more fun things and creative things." She spent "too much time" on discipline in the basic class and found that the students "hated" reading; they had little interest in what she was teaching. She said she was more able to be herself with the high-ability students. In the final analysis, this teacher's ideas on tracking had more to do with her own comfort level than with the learning needs and opportunities of her students.

Demographic Differences: Urban, Suburban, and Rural Classes

In our study, the urban classes tended to be more lifeless than the suburban and rural classes. In interviews, the suburban teachers tended to sound more progressive than the practices we actually observed in their classes. The rural teachers had often taught the siblings and sometimes even the parents of their students, and they tended to view school as an extension of their students' families.

Urban Classes. Eighth-grade urban students in our study were involved in far fewer interactions with their teachers than either suburban or rural students; for the most part, the urban teachers seemed to "manage" students more than teach them in any conventional way. This was probably not due to large class sizes in urban schools since the average number of students (22) in these classes was only slightly greater than in either suburban (20) or rural (19) schools. Rather, instruction in urban schools seems to have suffered because the teachers in them were tired and burned out by the difficulties of dealing with challenging administrative and disciplinary problems, and felt as abandoned by their school systems as the children they taught.

In interviews, urban teachers frequently cited problems of truancy and attendance, discipline, short attention spans, general apathy and disengagement, and poor reading skills. A common attitude was that students "didn't particularly care" and "just did what they needed to do to get by—these kids don't bring pencil and paper half the time." These complaints even extended to some academically talented students, who, according to one teacher, were the "roughest kids in the school" and had "the attention span of a pea . . . they giggle at things even my lower-ability kids wouldn't react to." Some saw links between reading and discipline problems: "That is why you have so many struggling, so many failing, and so many discipline problems."

These teachers frequently felt orphaned along with their students by lack of support from central administration. Teachers said their schools spent little money, and even rationed paper. They felt stymied by large classes. One teacher said,

The numbers will kill you. The numbers! You're not going to *teach* 26. That's a big class.

Another teacher said her school system had been

> very remiss in coming up with a plan for these basic kids. In fact, there isn't one. So all they have done is throw these materials at us, and no one has ever sat down and said, "Look, this is what you should cover. This is what these kids should know," or whatever. They pretty much leave it to the teacher. And if you went to other schools in the district, they would be doing something totally different. It's a very poor setup for these kids. And they are the ones that need the most structure, and they are not getting it.

Discouraged, these teachers often set remarkably low expectations for their students. They said they needed books with shorter chapters, lower-level vocabulary, and higher interest levels. One teacher said that morning was the best time to teach because her students' concentration was highest and she had fewer behavioral problems then. Students were more likely to be alert and fresh; there were "no clowns to disturb anyone." Even though her first-period class did not do much work, she nonetheless judged it to be a good one because the students were obedient and "did what they were told," and many of the troublemakers were "not alert enough to be disruptive." Absenteeism was high, and one-third of her students were usually late. Fridays were always the hardest day of the week. Discussion was hard. Most readings in the curriculum were irrelevant to students' lives. More than anything, this teacher said, she wanted her students to know she cared about them. After that, discipline — coming to class, doing the work, and following directions — was her most important goal.

Yet not all urban teachers had given up. One teacher, specially trained to teach Title I students, was upbeat. She liked her students and found the remediation techniques she had learned highly effective. She reported no significant discipline problems and found parents cooperative. She especially favored small-group work because there "you can really discuss." She liked using newspapers because "you could discuss recent developments," and she claimed success when she asked students to write questions about what they were learning. Another teacher emphasized that it was up to her as the teacher to "discern gifts, bring out students, make them grow," and that she was able to do this. She looked at students as individuals — "people working with me" — and her students often came back just to "talk about life." She allowed regular time for "impromptu sessions," and said students became engaged when she took the time to ask, "What do you think of this?" Another teacher stressed the importance of respect: "Teaching has got to be respectful. And you have to establish that rapport early because the anger and hostility are very difficult to wear off once they start."

Nonetheless, most of the teachers in the urban schools said discussion and small-group work were impossible. They generally had resigned themselves to worksheets and newspapers as the best they could offer. Most just tried to keep order in their classrooms, especially through seatwork, which was the dominant mode of instruction, averaging more than 21 minutes a day. On top of this, eighth-grade urban teachers lectured about 6 minutes a day. Even question–answer exchanges involved too much interaction for these teachers, and it averaged only about 9 minutes a day versus 14 minutes for suburban students and nearly 19 minutes for rural students. Unsurprisingly, discussion was rare in these classes, averaging only 45 seconds a day.

Eighth-grade urban teachers asked about as many authentic questions (13%) as suburban teachers did (12%) but twice as many as rural teachers (6%). In ninth-grade classes, these differences were even more pronounced: 33% of teacher questions asked in urban classes were authentic compared with 22% in suburban classes and 9% in rural classes, although in a subsequent analysis (see p. 58), we discovered that many authentic questions did not concern literature or anything academic. Tables 2.5 and 2.6 summarize these and other data.

In grade 9, seatwork in urban classes diminished to about 7 minutes a day, whereas lecture increased to almost 9 minutes a day and question–answer increased to 18. This was the case even though, unlike the eighth-grade classes, the average number of students in ninth-grade urban classes (about 25) was notably higher than either suburban (22) or rural (19) classes. Tables 2.4 and 2.6 summarize these and additional data.

Suburban Classes. Most suburban teachers in our sample said they prized student autonomy: the ability and willingness to articulate and defend ideas. The suburban teachers were clearly more up-to-date on leading-edge pedagogy and professional buzzwords than were the urban teachers. The fundamental province of their instruction, as they saw it, was the life of the mind. Discussion commonly was cited as a goal for all classes; one teacher represented the expressed views of the others when he said, "It is important for students to participate, to feel free to voice their opinions, to present divergent opinions without feeling intimidated, to do the work, be motivated, and be free and willing to discuss literature." His goals for students were excitement and depth of understanding. Another teacher wanted all his students to "discuss, contribute, and offer original ideas."

In fact, we observed more teacher–student interaction in the suburban than in the urban schools, especially in eighth-grade classes. The suburban teachers did less lecturing than the urban (4 minutes a day versus 6), and their students did less seatwork (15 minutes a day versus more than 21). Yet "discussion" in these schools was rarely open-ended and generally took the form of question-and-answer recitation: Eighth-grade suburban classes typically had more than 14 minutes a day of question–answer activities versus less than 10 minutes in urban classes, and actual discussion was about 50 seconds a day on average, not much more than in urban schools. In ninth-grade suburban classes, we encountered not even a second of discussion.

If suburban teachers prized student autonomy and independent thought, they also said they prized sharing and cooperation. Many teachers used small groups to promote such values, and in both eighth- and ninth-grade classes, suburban students spent twice as much time as urban students in small groups.

Reading skills of suburban students were stronger than those of urban students, and this difference was evident in the fact that suburban students spent less time reading aloud in class. The eighth-grade classes spent about 2½ minutes a day reading aloud compared with more than 3 minutes a day in the urban classes; in the ninth-grade classes, this difference became even more pronounced: The suburban classes spent only 43 seconds reading aloud, whereas urban classes spent more than 2 minutes. While urban teachers often sought simplified reading materials, suburban teachers sometimes did just the opposite. As one told us, "Last year I used a basic reader. . . . There were good stories, but they were so watered down that I said I can't use this book. I realize that the stuff I use now, the kids are frustrated with the vocabulary, but that's life." The suburban teachers said they spent more time on interpretation than on reading skills. They told us they encouraged students to give opinions, explain why, and go "beyond remembering" to "using" texts. Yet the cognitive level of questions asked in eighth-grade suburban classes was no higher than in urban classes, and in ninth grade it was actually lower. Nor did suburban teachers ask more authentic questions: In eighth grade, about 12–13% of all teacher questions were authentic in both suburban and urban classes; in ninth grade, urban teachers asked about 50% more. Tables 2.3–2.6 summarize these and other data.

Rural Classes. Schools in small, rural towns were a lot like the towns themselves — places where everybody knew everybody and where secrets could sometimes be hard to keep. Teachers often knew the siblings of their students and kept in close touch with the parents: One teacher regularly recognized his students as "chips off the ol' block." Because the same students often spent the day together through all their classes, they often knew each other's grades, and this was sometimes a problem. Also, because the schools were so small, there was often no ability grouping; everyone was just mixed together. Virtually all the teachers approved of this. They felt that "the slower kids don't learn as much if they're grouped," and believed that mixed groups provided these students with role models. They also said it was important for the smarter kids to "learn the other side of life."

Teachers told us they prized "question-and-answer discussion," which averaged approximately 18 minutes a day in both eighth and ninth grades. We found more open-ended discussion in eighth-grade rural classes than in any of the other schools, on average a little less than 2 minutes a day. Also, seatwork in grade 8 occupied much less time in rural than in urban and suburban schools. Tables 2.3–2.6 summarize these and other data.

ANALYZING THE DATA: THE EFFECTS OF DISCOURSE ON LEARNING

How concerned should we be with these bleak figures? Our data enabled us to test specific hypotheses concerning the overall effects of dialogic elements on learning. There is clearly a trade-off between research, such as our study, that comprehensively depicts the big picture and examines general effects, on the one hand, and case studies that examine the dynamics of individual cases and episodes, on the other. Ideally these different perspectives complement each other. Our large study enabled us to test empirically many widely debated hypotheses about the effectiveness of different instructional practices and discourse environments (e.g., recitation, discussion, small-group work) for learning.

In a series of analyses, we examined the effects of many of these practices on literature achievement. To assess student learning, we administered a literature test in the spring to each class. The test required students to answer a series of questions about five works of literature (stories, novels, dramas, and short plays) they had read during the year.[14] The questions ranged from simple recall (e.g., "Who were the main characters in *Roll of Thunder, Hear My Cry?*") to ones requiring in-depth understanding ("Relate the conflict of *Roll of Thunder, Hear My Cry* to the ending and to the theme"). The same types of questions were asked of each class, but the stories varied, depending on what students actually read during the year. For the ninth-grade test students also wrote a brief essay on a character from their reading whom they admired. An example of an eighth-grade test is found in Appendix A.

The literature tests were scored for the following:

1. Extent of recall
2. Depth of understanding
3. Number of endings remembered
4. Relation of ending to denouement
5. Relation of conflict/and or ending to theme

6. Understanding of the internal motivations of characters
7. Interpretive treatment of the major selection
8. Level of discourse used to discuss theme and conflict

Readers read the entire test and then determined a single score for each of the above variables. Each student's literature score was the sum of the individual scores. Each test was scored by two readers and the scores were averaged. The overall reliability of the assessment in grade 8, computed as a correlation of the two readings, was .90; in the grade 9 assessment, the reliability was .82. The rubric used for scoring the tests is shown in Appendix B.

We then examined the effects of instruction and classroom discourse on learning through a statistical technique called regression analysis. Regression analysis makes it possible to examine the effect of one condition (e.g., the amount of time spent in discussion) while statistically holding constant other important conditions (e.g., prior abilities in writing and reading, socioeconomic status, and characteristics of students in different classes). For example, if authentic questions are found to be related to higher achievement, regression analysis can reveal whether this is because teachers ask previously higher-achieving students more authentic questions, or whether authentic questions actually promote higher achievement. Regression analyses systematically estimate the effect of each variable while statistically holding constant each of the other variables. Our analyses controlled for the effects of both background variables (sex, race, ethnicity, family socioeconomic status) and prior achievement (as measured by fall tests of reading and writing skills).[15]

Overall Results

In none of our analyses did we ever find that a higher cognitive level of instructional activities actually enhanced learning. Instead, we could explain the relative effectiveness of different instructional practices only when we examined the ways teachers and students interacted as evidenced by authentic questions, uptake, and especially discussion.

Eighth-Grade Classes. The results of our analyses of the eighth-grade classes, controlled for writing and reading ability, socioeconomic status (SES), race, and ethnicity, showed unsurprisingly that disengagement, including off-task behavior and failure to complete homework, adversely affected achievement. The results revealed a modest effect for time spent on homework, no effect for how many questions were asked in class, and a negative effect for level of activity during recitation. Results indicated that dialogically organized instruction, indicated by time devoted to discussion, authentic questions, uptake, and high-level teacher evaluation, had a strong, positive effect on achievement. Discussion in particular had a large effect, which is especially striking when it is recalled that the average class engaged in less than a minute of discussion each day. Table 2.7 summarizes these results.

In our eighth-grade study, we also found that effective teachers of literature regularly assigned extended pieces of exposition (Nystrand, 1991c); this practice enhanced students' recall and understanding of the literary works they read. The frequent assignment of short-answer exercises, however, actually degraded students' overall recall and depth of understanding. This result is consistent with Applebee's (1984) contention that, because writing tends to promote recall of what it focuses on, such "narrow-banded" activities as short-answer exercises are likely to hinder total recall — in other words, helping students to remember trees at the expense of understanding the overall shape of the forest. In addition, because they elicit cryptic, fragmented discourse, short-answer exercises promote superficial involvement with literature; in so doing, they trivialize students' experiences with literature. All in all, students learn literature best in classes that encourage substantive and personal student response to literature in both classroom interaction and writing. Table 2.8 summarizes the results.

Ninth-Grade Classes. In analyzing data from the ninth grade (Gamoran & Nystrand, 1992), we sought to replicate our findings from the eighth-grade study, but we were initially frustrated to find that discussion had no effect on learning in ninth grade and that authentic questions appeared to have no effect or even a negative effect. We were further perplexed to discover that authentic questions had positive effects in high-track classes but negative effects in low-track classes. Table 2.9 summarizes these results.

Looking more closely at our data, we discovered that the two different tracks used authentic questions very differently. In the high-track classes, fully 68% of authentic questions concerned literature, whereas only 25% of authentic questions in low-track classes did. In low-track classes, teachers' authentic questions often concerned such issues as, "How do most of you feel about tests?"; "What would your parents say if you got an A on next week's test?"; "What things would you associate with lying in the sun?"; "Do you ever have to take notes?" Discussion broke down in a similar way so that discussion in the high-track classes tended to be about literature far more than did that in the low-track classes.

Tracking, Instructional Discourse, and Learning

Again and again, researchers have found that tracking and ability grouping promote inequality of achievement, as the gap between students in high-track and low-track classes widens over time (Gamoran & Berends, 1987).

Table 2.7. Effects of Disengagement, Procedural Engagement, and Substantive Engagement on Spring Literature Achievement in Grade 8 (metric regression coefficients)

		Model		
Independent Variable	Background Variables Only	Procedural Engagement Variables	Substantive Engagement Variables	Full Model (All Variables)
Background				
Sex (1 = female)	0.44	0.47	0.62[*]	0.59[*]
	(0.38)	(0.36)	(0.35)	(0.34)
Race (1 = Black)	-2.67[****]	-1.55[**]	-1.75[****]	-1.10[*]
	(0.66)	(0.64)	(0.62)	(0.61)
Ethnicity (1 = Hispanic)	-1.51[**]	-0.15	-1.47[**]	-0.58
	(0.64)	(0.62)	(0.60)	(0.59)
SES	1.62[****]	1.10[****]	1.45[****]	1.05[****]
	(0.24)	(0.24)	(0.23)	(0.23)
Grade (1 = eighth)	2.09[****]	1.10[*]	1.11[**]	0.16
	(0.57)	(0.56)	(0.57)	(0.56)
Fall reading score	0.39[****]	0.30[****]	0.36[****]	0.30[****]
	(0.04)	(0.04)	(0.04)	(0.04)
Fall writing score	0.93[****]	0.70[****]	0.73[****]	0.58[****]
	(0.15)	(0.14)	(0.14)	(0.14)
Disengagement				
Off task in class		-0.23[****]		-0.16[****]
		(0.03)		(0.03)
Reading not completed		-0.02		-0.02[*]
		(0.01)		(0.01)
Writing not completed		-0.03[***]		0.02[**]
		(0.01)		(0.01)
Nonresponse to questions		-0.20[****]		-0.22[****]
		(0.06)		(0.06)
Procedural engagement				
Active in class		-0.03[**]		-0.06[****]
		(0.02)		(0.02)
Asking questions		-0.02		-0.03
		(0.02)		(0.02)
Time on homework		0.45[***]		0.38[**]
		(0.17)		(0.16)
Substantive engagement				
Authentic questions			0.05[****]	0.04[**]
			(0.02)	(0.02)
Authentic reading			-0.01	0.02
			(0.03)	(0.03)
High evaluation of writing			-0.39	-0.03
			(0.40)	(0.40)
Uptake			0.14[****]	0.10[***]
			(0.03)	(0.03)
Coherence of reading			0.16[****]	0.11[****]
			(0.03)	(0.03)
Discussion time			0.34[***]	0.29[***]
			(0.11)	(0.11)
Small- group time			-0.19[**]	-0.23[****]
			(0.07)	(0.07)
R^2	.322	.399	.428	.475

Source: Nystrand & Gamoran, 1991a.
Notes: Dependent variable: Spring Literature Achievement Test. $N = 924$ students. Missing values deleted listwise. Numbers in parentheses are standard errors.
* $p < .10$ (marginal trend) ** $p < .05$ *** $p < .01$ **** $p < .001$

Table 2.8. Effects of Selected Instructional Variables on Difficulty of Recall and Difficulty of Understanding Literature in Depth in Grade 8 (metric regression coefficients)

	Difficulty of Recall	Difficulty of Understanding in Depth
Background variables		
Grade (1 = eighth)	0.054	-0.183
	(0.090)	(0.118)
Race (1 = Black)	0.246	0.068
	(0.091)	(0.120)
Ethnicity (1 = Hispanic)	0.122	0.165
	(0.089)	(0.117)
SES	-0.107****	-0.138***
	(0.036)	(0.048)
Sex (1 = female)	-0.120**	-0.174*
	(0.052)	(0.069)
Fall writing score	-0.073****	-0.105****
	(0.021)	(0.027)
Fall reading score	-0.034****	-0.036****
	(0.005)	(0.007)
Procedural variables		
Time on homework	-0.065***	-0.058*
	(0.024)	(0.031)
Reading not completed	0.0004	0.0004
	(0.002)	(0.003)
Writing not completed	0.005**	0.002**
	(0.002)	(0.003)
Participation in class	-0.001	-0.001
	(0.002)	(0.002)
No response to teacher questions	0.008	0.026*
	(0.010)	(0.013)
Instructional variables		
Amount of writing	-0.256**	-0.289**
	(0.104)	(0.137)
Discussion time	-0.022	-0.038*
	(0.016)	(0.022)
Authenticity of teacher questions	-0.0005	-0.006**
	(0.002)	(0.003)
Authenticity of readings	-0.003	-0.018***
	(0.005)	(0.006)
Uptake	-0.015****	-0.020****
	(0.005)	(0.006)
Relating discussions to other discussions and student compositions	0.005	0.001
	(0.004)	(0.005)
Relating readings to other readings	-0.046**	-0.018
	(0.019)	(0.025)
R^2	.353	.339

Source: Nystrand, 1991c.
Notes: $N = 762$ students. Missing values deleted listwise. Numbers in parentheses are standard errors.
* $p < .10$ (marginal trend)   ** $p < .05$ *** $p < .01$ **** $p < .001$

Table 2.9. Effects of Instruction and Engagement on Ninth-Grade Literature Achievement

Variable	Mean	SD	Regression Coefficient	SE
Background variables				
Sex (1 = female)	0.51	0.50	1.47**	0.37
Race (1 = black)	0.07	0.26	-0.46	0.72
Ethnicity (1 = Hispanic)	0.09	0.28	-1.56*	0.65
SES	-0.02	0.80	0.44	0.25
Fall reading score	31.88	5.34	0.40**	0.04
Fall writing score	5.71	1.28	0.90**	0.15
Ability groups				
Honors/accelerated	0.24	0.43	0.25	0.96
Basic/remedial	0.10	0.30	-1.09	1.13
Other[a]	0.09	0.29	0.57	1.16
Psychological engagement				
Engagement scale[b]	2.42	1.40	0.02	0.14
Behavioral engagement				
Writing completed	87.88%	19.68	0.03**	0.01
Reading completed	83.04%	24.62	0.03**	0.01
Homework time (hrs/wk)	1.27	1.27	0.19	0.15
Off task in class	3.22%	3.27	-0.12*	0.06
Instructional discourse				
Authentic questions				
In honors classes	24.30%	11.41	0.10**	0.03
In regular classes	28.13%	18.81	-0.02	0.01
In remedial classes	27.40%	18.86	-0.09**	0.04
In other classes	36.90%	26.03	-0.20**	0.03
Uptake	25.90%	11.26	0.09**	0.02
Discussion (min/day)	0.24	0.48	-0.18	0.40
Coherence[c]	13.01	7.07	0.12**	0.03

Source: Gamoran & Nystrand, 1992.

Notes: N = 971 students. Dependent variable: Spring Literature Achievement Test (mean = 21.82, SD = 7.66). R^2 = .52.

[a] Other classes include two classes in a school-within-a-school program and two classes in a heterogeneously grouped school.

[b] Engagement scale based on student responses to the following questions, coded on a weekly scale: In English class, how often do you: (a) Try as hard as you can? (b) Think what you are learning is interesting and worthwhile? (c) Find yourself concentrating so hard that time passes quickly?

[c] Coherence measure based on teacher responses to the following questions, coded on a weekly scale: (a) About how often do students in your class write about (or in response to) things they have read? (b) About how often do you discuss writing topics with your students before asking them to write? (c) About how often do you and your class discuss the readings you assign? (d) When you ask students about their reading assignments in class, how frequently do you attempt to do each of the following: Ask them to relate what they have read to their other readings? (e) About how often does your class relate its discussion to previous discussions you have had? (f) About how often do you and your class discuss things students have written about?

* $p < .05$ ** $p < .01$

A major purpose of our investigation was to determine whether inequality resulted from differences in the quality of discourse in high-track and low-track classes. This question is not easy to answer, for two reasons. First, prior to our study, quantitative measures of discourse quality had not been available. Second, it is hard to measure the effects of tracking because they are confounded with initial differences among students. Students assigned to different tracks have different achievement from the start, and it is important to take this into account when examining inequality.

We addressed the first problem by developing the scheme for measuring classroom discourse described in this chapter. We addressed the second problem with statistical controls for fall reading and writing skills, as well as controls for sex, race/ethnicity, and SES (see note 15). In addition, for this analysis, we used standardized reading and math test scores as indicators of an underlying "ability" construct, to add a stricter control for students' prior academic background (Gamoran et al., 1995). Even with these controls, we found that average achievement was almost two points higher in honors classes than in remedial classes, a statistically significant difference. One standard deviation on the test was 6.8 points, so the two-point gap was almost 30% of a standard deviation, a substantial amount (Gamoran et al., 1995).

Do differences in instructional discourse account for this achievement inequality? Yes, to a large extent (Gamoran et al., 1995). Part of the difference occurred because students in honors classes were more responsive — they completed more of their reading and writing assignments — which helped them learn more (see Table 2.10). Uptake and discourse coherence also helped students learn, but these did not account for track differences in learning, because they occurred at similar rates in honors and remedial classes (see Tables 2.5 and 2.6). Authentic questions also were comparably distributed across class types, but they were beneficial only in honors classes because there they pertained to literature (see Table 2.10). Hence, similar levels of authenticity led to inequality of learning, because the content of the authentic questions differed.

We further observed that students were more often off task in remedial classes, and this was detrimental to their achievement (see Table 2.10). In honors classes, where off-task behavior was less prevalent, its effects were less harmful. Conversely, discussion occurred more often in honors classes, where it brought benefits for literature achievement, and had no benefits in other classes, presumably because it focused on topics other than literature.

These results contradicted the usual rationale for ability grouping. Ability grouping is supposed to allow teachers and students to engage in whatever instruction is most beneficial in each context. In actuality, we found that authentic questions occurred at similar rates in all classes, but contributed to achievement only in honors classes; off-task behavior was most common

Table 2.10. Maximum Likelihood Estimates of Background and Instructional Effects on Literature Achievement in Eighth- and Ninth-Grade Ability-Grouped English Classes

Independent Variable	Effect	SE
Background		
Sex (1 = female)	1.188[a]	0.252
Minority (1 = Black or Hispanic)	−0.652	0.339
SES	0.155	0.174
Fall reading score	0.202[a]	0.024
Fall writing score	0.512[a]	0.103
Ability	0.121[a]	0.018
Instruction		
Completion of reading	0.022[b]	0.006
Completion of writing	0.025[b]	0.007
Off task in class		
Honors classes	0.149	0.092
Regular classes	−0.193[a]	0.044
Remedial classes	−0.124[a]	0.028
Authentic teacher questions		
Honors classes	0.056[c]	0.022
Regular classes	0.000	0.010
Remedial classes	−0.050[c]	0.017
Uptake	0.063[a]	0.013
Discussion		
Honors classes	0.277[c]	0.129
Regular classes	−1.510[c]	0.591
Remedial classes	0.045	0.169
Discourse coherence	0.158[a]	0.022
Intercepts		
Honors classes	−8.502[a]	1.385
Regular classes	−7.081[a]	1.207
Remedial classes	−7.144[a]	1.061

χ^2 (61, N = 1,564) = 86.33

Source: Gamoran et al., 1995
[a] Coefficient is four times its standard error.
[b] Coefficient is three times its standard error.
[c] Coefficient is twice its standard error.

where it was most harmful, in regular and remedial classes. Discussion fit the pattern of occurring more where its payoff was greater (in honors classes); this, too, contributed to inequality.

In light of these results, we concluded that two changes must be considered (Gamoran et al., 1995). Either ability grouping in eighth- and ninth-grade English should be eliminated, or it should be implemented very differently than typically occurs at present. To mitigate the inequality that results from grouping and tracking, teachers and students in regular and low-level classes need higher expectations and more engaging discourse that focuses on academic subject matter.

Small Groups

In the eighth-grade study, we initially expected small groups to be dependable sites of dialogic peer interaction, but this was naive. In fact, time spent in small groups, rare as it was — 39 seconds a day on average — turned out to have a prominent negative effect on achievement. We had predicted that small-group work and discussion would enhance achievement by engaging students substantively, especially compared with lecture, drill work, and recitation, which, like short-answer study questions, typically involve abbreviated responses from students. In fact, increased time spent in small-group work seemed to result in lower achievement in literature. We decided to examine this finding in more detail in a follow-up study of ninth-grade literature classes. We were particularly interested in distinguishing various kinds of small-group work and to see whether some were more effective than others.

In the ninth-grade study, unlike the eighth-grade study, we audiotaped the classes we observed, and although we had not placed microphones in small groups, the tapes provided a record of how each class proceeded. For classes involving small-group work, we were able to determine: (a) what preceded and what followed this work, (b) the kinds of tasks undertaken in groups, (c) the instructions the teachers gave to the groups, and (d) the roles teachers played in setting up and running the groups.

We learned that small-group work involved a great range of activities. Some small-group work was so highly structured by the teacher — involving, for example, students completing worksheets together — that it might best be called "collaborative seatwork." Other groups, which we called problem-solving groups, required students to come to consensus concerning some issue or question that the teacher defined. Yet other small-group work, which we described as "autonomous," was even more open-ended, with the groups themselves defining as well as resolving the problems and issues they discussed. Figure 2.2 shows the continuum described by these categories.

Our study looked exclusively at the features of small-group work that promote thinking. Given our findings that ownership, coherence of discourse, and student production of knowledge are important features of effective instruction, we reasoned that to promote response to and thinking about literature, small groups also should manifest these traits. More specifically, we predicted that collaborative seatwork, which is essentially written recitation done by students working together, would be less effective than problem-

Figure 2.2. Continuum of Small-Group Work

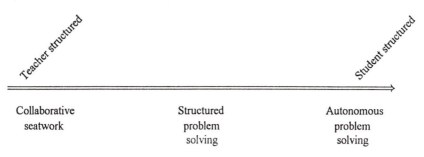

Collaborative	Structured	Autonomous
seatwork	problem	problem
	solving	solving

solving and autonomous groups, which allow ownership and thereby maximize the possibility of coherent discussion. It may be that collaborative seatwork is effective for teaching facts and grammar, but our research did not examine this possibility.

As we examined the range of activities that we had coded as small-group work, we confirmed our initial impression that "small-group time" was a misleading category because of important differences among the activities that occurred in small groups. We can illustrate these contrasting activities by focusing on two dimensions of work in small groups: student autonomy and student production of knowledge. Small-group activities occurred in only 29 of the 216 class sessions we observed. The small-group sessions averaged about 15 minutes when they occurred, but because they were so infrequent, small-group time accounted for less than 2 minutes of the average 50-minute period among all the classes. The groupwork we observed was usually closer to collaborative seatwork than to student problem-solving and autonomous groupwork.

Student Autonomy. Teachers shape groupwork by assigning tasks and establishing parameters of interaction. In highly "prescribed" groupwork, the parameters are defined entirely by the teacher, and the task could just as easily be done without interaction among students. The group setting is gratuitous, used perhaps more for the teacher's convenience. Here is an example from a ninth-grade English class.

Today while you are working in groups you will keep the same groups that you had yesterday. The same rules will apply, and those are: You must, as a group, form a tight circle; you must bring all of your materials with you to that group and you may NOT get up from your seat; your voice must stay at a whisper—if I can hear you above anyone else's, that means you are too loud and your name will go up on the

board. You may do one of two things in your group. You may continue
to work on your paper—there are five, probably six people I have to see
yet in conference. If you are as far as you can go in your groups with
your papers—that is, editing, proofreading, all of those—then as a
group, I would like you to see if you can fill in the blanks on this handout on five basic sentence patterns: how to find them, what questions
to ask. And we will go over this. Remember one section of your binders
should be sentence patterns.

This groupwork, so completely structured by the teacher, promotes neither
ownership nor coherent discussion.

In more autonomous groups, the teacher gives students some latitude in
their interactions with each other, and although students may remain on a
"short leash," the groupwork nonetheless displays spontaneous student interactions concerning the substance of the lesson. In the most autonomous
groups, the teacher clearly defines group tasks but without prescripting
the groupwork. Typically the teacher (a) defines the goal of the group, for
example, arriving at a consensus concerning some controversial issue; (b)
outlines the tasks to be accomplished, for example, the group composition
of a letter outlining the group's views to a public official; and/or (c) assigns
roles to group members, for example, two group members argue one side of
the issue while two others argue the other side and one student acts as the
recorder. In the following transcript, for example, the teacher initiates
groupwork after students have written some original verse. Referring to the
students' poems, the teacher says:

> If yours is the best it can be—instead of counting off, because we'll run
> out of time, will you just group together with the three or four—three
> or four maximum—people around you. Read them over, and choose
> the one [poem] that . . . looks the most specific to you—see that person
> that they're talking about.

A little later, this teacher reminds students that she wants

> to hear what you've picked out in your groups so that you're hearing
> some of the real strong images of these people. . . . I'm asking you to
> brag; I want to hear the three or four REAL good ones, so people who
> are having difficulty get a good sample before they go home.

This skillfully organized groupwork starts with expressive student writing,
thus promoting ownership. Not only because students must work together
to find good examples but also because the teacher encourages them to articu-

late what "good" means in this context, the ensuing group talk is more likely to be coherent conversation than the first session, where students must "fill in the blanks on this handout on five basic sentence patterns." Such discussions were rare in our study: Only 11.1% of all small-group work was judged either to be wholly autonomous or to display significant student interaction in producing the outcome of groupwork, whereas 70.4% of all small-group work was prestructured by the teacher.

The degree of student autonomy in the small groups we observed was coded from audiotapes according to the following scale:

1   *Teacher-structured groupwork:* Task parameters entirely defined, or "prescripted," by teacher. Task can be done without student interaction (e.g., worksheets); group setting is gratuitous.
2   *Prescripted task* with obligatory student interaction.
3   *Limited student interaction:* Groupwork involves spontaneous student interaction concerning substance but students are on "short leash." For example, the teacher might define some general principle that students in groups must then apply.
4   *Significant student interaction* defining shape of task and outcome, although teacher might have been able to predict results before class.
5   *Autonomous groupwork:* Teacher sets up groupwork without prescripting activities; significant student interaction define shape of task and outcome. Results of groupwork cannot be predicted before class.

Student Production of Knowledge. In addition to promoting coherent conversation, the second example encourages students to generate insights and understandings far more than the first session. In activities such as completing worksheets and answering study questions, students are required mainly to manipulate and master information provided by the teacher or a textbook. This work calls only for lower-order cognitive activity, characterized by questions with prespecified right and wrong answers, and it tends not to be very coherent because it does not build on student responses. It consequently fails to result in student production of knowledge. Here is an example.

Everyone put their name in the upper right. Put your name and your period and the group number in the upper right-hand corner. Now I've gone over two or three times your group number so you should remember it — when you get into your groups, if you have forgotten it, maybe somebody in there will remember it. Now you are to combine eight sentences to form the kind of sentence shown in parentheses, okay? And I mean that . . . when I say a simple sentence, that's what I mean: a

simple sentence that has one subject and one predicate. When I say com-
pound sentence, I mean two sentences of equal value and equal importance, put together with a conjunction or a semicolon or a transitive adverb, okay? Complex sentences: you will be asked to either write one
with an adjective clause or an adverb clause. And because there were no
noun clauses, I have given you a task down below here to write two sentences with noun clauses. Now, all of the sentences up above — the first
eight — are all about Niagara Falls and the river and stuff like that, and
though it isn't absolutely important that you focus on the Niagara
River, it would be kind of nice if you did it, all right?

In another example, from another class, the teacher puts students to work in
groups on a worksheet concerning Greek gods.

I know you won't finish the entire chart, but we will be starting . . .
sharing, because what we want to be sure is that everyone has the same
items on the chart. So I will give you the next 15 minutes . . . to just
work on what you have. Be sure if you haven't — some of you maybe
start from the back; we won't get them all checked today so that you
have the chart. This is the chart that you will have to memorize, you
will be tested on it . . . I want to make sure you all have the same information.

In both these examples, the groupwork involves little or no production of
knowledge. In other groups, by contrast, students must sustain a coherent
discussion in order to work out problems that generate new understandings.
Typically, this groupwork proceeds in response to open-ended questions with
more than one acceptable answer and involves higher-order cognitive activity.
In the following transcript, for example, the teacher asks students to predict
the ending of an Agatha Christie novel. To get them thinking, she first asks
them to write a brief plot summary.

In a paragraph, write out what happened, what you think happened —
and talk it out first, because there are a lot of lights going on in your
eyes, and some of you are still saying, "I have no idea." Get together
in your group, and on a sheet of loose-leaf tell me what happened.

As students work, the teachers says:

As I came around, a lot of you picked up a lot of the clues as to how
she might have been killed and, so then, who would have done it. Who-
ever you're accusing, think about a motive — so some of you are saying,

"Oh, the inspector did it," or "The colonel did it," or "Pollet did it," or "Ted did it," and that's all you're writing down. What I came around and asked you for was a motive, right? Miss Marple's got that down. So in your paragraph: who did it and a motive.

In another lesson, from another class, the teacher asks her students to analyze the characterization of Mr. Morrison in *Roll of Thunder, Hear My Cry*.

Here's what you need to do. . . . First of all, you want to name three outstanding character traits. Now, remember traits refer to personality, not physical characteristics. . . . Give supporting quotations for your ideas, one quote for each trait will be fine, and then give a warrant— that is, explain how the quote sets up that trait or how it establishes that trait, and then tell me what technique [the author] is using. Does she use a character's language, a character's actions, or do you see the character through the eyes of another character, or the reaction of another character?

In each of these latter two examples, students must not only identify some underlying principle—a motive for murder, a character trait—but also find supporting evidence for the interpretation. Once again, we discovered that such groupwork is infrequent; only about a quarter of the groupwork we observed involved discussion of open-ended questions with students actively constructing interpretations (rated a 5 on the scale in the list that follows). By contrast, two-thirds was a version of collaborative seatwork.

In our analysis of the extent to which students were required to actively construct new understandings during small-group work, we coded each session, using audiotapes, according to the following scale:

1   Collaborative seatwork. Students receive only prespecified information; student activities in small groups are tightly controlled. Worksheets are an example.
2   Students primarily receive prespecified information; occasionally their tasks involve open-ended questions. Student activities are highly orchestrated, with topic coverage defined by the teacher.
3   Teacher identifies issue or problem; students find examples and explore applications. Teacher provides time and encouragement for exploring new meanings and implications.
4   Students receive some information; much of the groupwork involves students using information with open-ended questions or with teacher-provided questions.
5   Students identify both problems and applications. Discussing open-

ended questions, students actively construct interpretations. Teacher sets the parameters of the groupwork, but it is mainly the students who work out ways to address issues and answer questions.

Effective and Ineffective Groupwork. Did small-group work affect achievement, holding other conditions constant? In our regression analysis, we held constant students' sex, race/ethnicity, SES, and fall reading and writing skills. We also took into account teachers' uses of authentic and follow-up questions, the amount of discussion time outside of small groups, as well as rates of student off-task behavior and homework completion.

We first discovered that, overall, classes spending more time in small groups produced lower achievement, a finding that replicated the surprising conclusion of our eighth-grade study. However, we were now prepared to go beyond simply asking how much time was spent in small groups: We could ask whether the effectiveness of small-group time depended on what was going on in the small groups. To do this, we used the two measures of the quality of group time discussed earlier: student autonomy and student production of knowledge. Although these measures differ in theory — students could be given autonomy but not take the opportunity to produce knowledge — in practice the two tended to occur together: the more student autonomy, the more production of knowledge (the correlation was .78).[16]

Analysis of student autonomy showed that the higher the degree of autonomy, the more likely group time was to contribute positively to achievement. For example, a class that averaged 5 minutes per day of highly "prescripted," rigidly structured group time, with little autonomy for students, would actually score about 1 point lower on the test than a class with no group time at all. By contrast, a class that averaged 5 minutes of highly autonomous groupwork, in which students worked together to define the task, would gain almost 2 points on the test over a similar class with no groupwork. This is a significant effect: It could move a student from the fiftieth to the fifty-eighth percentile on the 32-point test. We found similar results for student production of knowledge: Collaborative seatwork actually reduces achievement, but groupwork in which students actively construct interpretations promotes achievement.

These results are consistent with Hillocks's (1986) study, which examined dozens of empirical studies conducted over a quarter century involving nearly 12,000 students and found that the most effective writing instruction involved peer-response groups with what Hillocks called an "inquiry" focus: assigned topics involving analysis of readings or other data and attention to rhetorical strategies.

By replicating our eighth-grade study and moving beyond it, we accounted for the unexpected results. Small-group work appeared ineffective because the groups were being used ineffectively; many of the assignments could just as well have been done individually. The follow-up study shows that when small-group time allows students to interact over the substance of their problem, defining tasks as well as solutions and constructing interpretations, students benefit from the opportunity to work in small groups.[17]

These findings reaffirm the view that effective small-group work requires coherent activities that result in the sustained production of student knowledge. To promote such activities, the teacher must not overly specify group tasks. In other words, effective teachers clearly define the general parameters of the tasks, but not the precise character of the activities themselves. Teachers who promote thinking about literature may present clear objectives to students for groupwork — for example, identifying the best poems written by students in each group, articulating character traits, and finding supporting quotations — but avoid telling groups exactly how to proceed; they do not, for example, specify a list of questions and topics students must answer in a particular order.

When teachers put groups of students together to work on some problem, they send students an important message that developing their own thoughts is important. The teacher above who told her students, "There are a lot of lights . . . in your eyes," as she prepared them for groupwork sent exactly this message.

The benefits of direct instruction presumably result from higher on-task behavior when the teacher works directly with students. One could argue that this occurs when the instructional task is the same for both whole-class and small-group settings. For example, students may be more on task when they answer recitation questions as a whole class than when the recitation questions are assigned to small groups for written responses. Learning, in this example, may not differ or may be greater in the whole-class format. However, this format does not take advantage of the opportunities for intellectual collaboration that are made possible by the small-group setting. If the tasks are the same, one should expect little difference in achievement; the point of small-group instruction, however, should not be to assign the same tasks, but to design work that draws on the potential for cooperation and collaboration in the small group.

If successful small-group work depends on the teacher setting up open-ended rather than prescribed tasks and on the students having coherent conversations generating insights, then teachers must carefully match small-group work to suitable tasks. For example, if the objective for a given day requires presenting a lot of new information, a lecture is probably better than small-group work. If teachers want students to practice some particular skill, recitation and seatwork may be better than small-group work. On the other hand, if teachers want students to compare ideas, develop a train of thought, air differences, or arrive at a consensus on some controversial issue, then the forum of small groups may be just the right setting for most students to carry on intensive conversation and discussion, especially students who are too shy to say much in the larger setting of the whole class. Teachers must always remember, however, that they cannot just put students in groups and expect them to "go to it" with positive results. For groupwork to succeed, teachers must carefully design collaborative tasks that are interesting to students (and not just to the teacher). They also must be prepared to help students develop effective group skills; an excellent guide for teachers is Cohen's *Designing Groupwork* (1986).

THE BOTTOM LINE: LEARNING TO THINK REQUIRES EFFECTIVE INTERACTION

Most of the time when teachers ask students questions, they are not asking to be informed since they already know the answers themselves. When students are asked to recite for teachers who have no need to be informed, they produce "pseudo-discourse." Authentic discourse occurs only when some information or interpretive stance is really at issue. Only authentic discourse can engage students.

Yet the results of our study suggest that authentic questions, discussion, small-group work, and interaction, though important, do not categorically produce learning; indeed we observed many classes where this was not the case. We also found that recitation is not categorically ineffective; rather, its effectiveness varies depending on whether and how teachers expand IRE sequences. The underlying epistemology of classroom interaction defines the bottom line for learning: What ultimately counts is *the extent to which instruction requires students to think, not just report someone else's thinking.* As Leont'ev (1981) might put it, the pedagogical usefulness of each interaction needs to be gauged in terms of the particular activity or project involved and, more than this, the system of social relationships that support it. Authentic questions, discussion, and small-group work have important instructional potential, but unless they are used in relation to serious instructional goals and, more important, unless they assign significant and serious epistemic roles to students that the students themselves can value, they may be little more than pleasant diversions.

In one English class in our study, for example, students engaged in several ostensibly open-ended, imaginative writing tasks requiring them to write from the point of view of a pencil eraser or a bullet. Upon close inspection of these exercises and especially the teacher's responses to the papers, we eventually came to understand that, from the teacher's point of view, the content of student responses to these prompts — imaginative or not — was irrelevant; nearly the only thing the teacher responded to in his marginal comments was whether or not all words had been spelled correctly. As it happened, the students in this class understood the operational rubric for this exercise and played their roles more or less appropriately. However, the ostensible purpose (imaginative discourse) and the actual purpose (correct spelling) of the writing tasks significantly differed; the writers were not really speaking to a reader who was listening to what they were trying to say. These writing tasks were what Bloome and Argumedo (1983) call procedural displays. Students can be involved fully and substantively in reciprocal instruction only when the ostensible purpose of the discourse is the same as the actual purpose.

Generally, we may say that reciprocity in instruction occurs most often when students, as well as the teacher, have some input into and control over instructional discourse, and when their previous learning significantly affects the course of subsequent learning. This concept has been implemented in some elementary reading instruction by Palincsar and Brown (1984) in what they call *reciprocal teaching*. In reciprocal teaching, students take turns being the teacher. In other classrooms where students do not play the role of teacher, the teachers nonetheless honor the terms of reciprocity when they avoid prespecifying answers to their questions so that student answers potentially can affect subsequent questions and discussion. When teachers ask genuine questions of this sort, they treat students as full-fledged conversants.

This is not to suggest that the dialogicality of instruction can be judged in terms of the *how* of instruction — question–answer sequences evidenced in face-to-face interaction — alone. The study found that the *what* of instruction — the content and subject matter — is critical to learning as well. Authentic questions must challenge students to think and reflect on the consequences of their ideas, not just remember their past experiences. Teachers must prize vigorous discussion in dialogic classrooms, encouraging what Bakhtin (1981) calls the struggle of "contradictory opinions, points of view and value judgments" (p. 281). Bakhtin teaches us that meaning and therefore learning — understood as the expansion of a personally coherent interpretation of information and events — are actively constructed and negotiated through language use. Learning is a dialogic event, part the instructor's and part the learner's. If events and information are to acquire meaning and students are to learn, then teachers must think of curriculum not just in terms of points to be made, information to be conveyed, and abstract skills to be mastered. Rather, they must engage students in activities and projects bridging the purposes of their students and the goals of instruction. Yet instruction creating such bridges, we found, was either rare or altogether missing in the classes we observed, which overwhelmingly were given over to lecture, recitation, short-answer questions, and seatwork.

The Bakhtinian explanation for the relative ineffectiveness of monologic instruction in promoting learning and conceptual change, compared with discussion and instructional conversation (even for basic objectives such as recall and literal comprehension), is that meaning "is realized only in the process of active, responsive understanding" (Vološinov, 1973, p. 102). Yet it is just such active, responsive understanding that teachers fail to practice — especially in low-track classes — when they determine prior to a given class the entire sequence of questions they will ask and what answers they will accept, and when they respond to correct student answers with a mere nod before moving on to the next question, often changing the topic of discourse. In doing so, these individuals make no attempt at active, responsive understanding; they "want, in effect, to turn on a light bulb after having switched off the current. Only the current of verbal intercourse endows a word with the light of meaning" (Vološinov, 1973, p. 103).

A Closer Look at Authentic Interaction: Profiles of Teacher–Student Talk in Two Classrooms

Robert Kachur and Catherine Prendergast

WHAT WAS GOING ON in Ms. Jansen's class? She seemed to ask open-ended questions that would allow students to bring in their own contributions, but her students were obviously, and increasingly loudly, unengaged. Off-task chatter grew more overwhelming as the literature session we were listening to progressed.

Ms. Jansen's class was one of a handful that seemed to contradict our overall finding that dialogic classrooms marked by ostensibly authentic teacher questions foster learning. Although classroom discourse in her class was characterized by 63% authentic teacher questions, the literature test scores were far lower than we had predicted, based on students' prior performance and socioeconomic status (SES).[1] What other factors were at work here? We began to wonder: Are the conditions that determine whether a productive dialogue between teacher and student can take place really within the teacher's control—and, if so, to what degree?

To explore these questions, we expanded our study to examine not just teacher questions, but also the teacher–student dialogue surrounding the questions. This approach seemed more in keeping with our theoretical rationale that dialogic instruction encourages student learning. After all, no study of the workings of dialogism in the classroom would be complete without incorporating analysis of actual dialogue; significant classroom interactions between students and teacher do not consist of question-and-answer exchanges alone.

SEARCHING FOR THE RIGHT ANSWERS

In all, 42 of the 66 questions asked by Ms. Jansen in this ninth-grade literature class were coded as authentic; thus, we expected to hear what a dialogic classroom sounded like when we listened to the audiotapes. In fact, some of the questions she posed to her 28 students about the short stories they had read were quite promising: "What is the difference between the words used by the children and the father?"; "How does that make you feel about words the children used?" Her comments, as well as her questions, seemed designed to elicit her students' feelings and views about what they were reading and thereby bring their voices into the discussion. For example:

> I told you yesterday that there are a lot of right answers. As I said, there are lot of different answers. And even my answers, I guessed on a lot of these, too. It's not specifically stated, so I'm assuming that you guessed, too. And we should come up with a bunch of different things.

When students did venture to answer her appeals for their contributions, however, their input was given only passing consideration.

> STUDENT 1: Well, Norton . . .
> Ms. JANSEN (interrupting): I have on the board Norton's name, now on this sheet, it means "what was most important to him or her."
> STUDENT 1: Norton's always beating up on people . . .
> Ms. JANSEN: Okay, what was most important? Okay, beating up on people . . .
> STUDENT 2: Beer.
> Ms. JANSEN: Okay, that's almost most important. What are the other ideas? That's not exclusively the answer. You could have other things down here. John?
> JOHN: Himself.
> STUDENT 3 (to another student): What was the first answer?
> Ms. JANSEN: Himself. That's a good answer.

Here, the teacher's attempt to build a dialogic environment by placing herself on the same level with the students (e.g., her admission, "There are a lot of right answers. . . . I guessed on a lot of these, too") is quickly undermined by the pattern of interruptions and hasty evaluations that characterizes the exchange. The statement, "That's almost most important," in response to a student's contribution, makes it clear that authenticity here is only ostensible, that there are in fact a limited number of right answers. Furthermore, she responded to the next student's contribution by saying, "That's a good answer," thereby closing off the conversation with an evaluation. By failing to encourage the students to elaborate their answers with a why-question, she missed many opportunities for a discussion that might have produced new thoughts on the material. In fact, her obvious search for "the right answer" encourages what Susan Hynds (1991) calls a "reductionistic perspective" that ultimately "turns students away from issues of interpretive complexity" (p. 118). The teacher's concern to come up with the best answers for the quiz questions may very well become the students' concern as they read.

Examining Ms. Jansen's comments as she set the tone for her class reveals what looking at her questions alone does not: The goal of the class session was not at all to foster genuine conversation. It is apparent from the very outset that her agenda was recitation, not dialogue. Her opening comments make clear that the answers to her questions were predetermined.

> Okay, we're going to go over yesterday's study guide from the quiz. I don't have your quiz scores recorded, although I have them graded, so I'll get your quizzes out, and if you guys can't remember I'll just look off your quizzes, to start the discussion.

This class was not only a review session; it was a review of a review session. What took place during the class period was no more cognitively taxing than an exercise of memory. Her suggestion that it doesn't even matter whether the students can "remember" the answers they've already written sends a strong message to the students that there will be no new knowledge created during this class session. Given this classroom context, students were hard pressed to consider any question the teacher asked as genuinely "authentic."

The recitation approach of sticking to initiation-response-evaluation (IRE) instructional scripts (see Chapter 1), and avoiding questions that might encourage interpretive complexity, effectively controls the knowledge produced in the class; it may, however, not effectively control the class itself. Despite the rigid format, this class was generally noisy and unruly. The din of students talking to each other clearly revealed that few were engaged by the question-and-answer format. In fact, we would maintain that the din was largely a *result* of the question-and-answer format. These students were quick to recognize that the teacher's questions were inauthentic and quick to lose patience with them. The more evident it became that any input that did not pertain to the exercise was not valued, the less attention they were willing to give the task at hand. Consequently, students' authentic voices surfaced in "unofficial" class activity — that is, off-task chatter (see Table 3.1). This is one example of what Bakhtin (1981) means when he suggests that manifestations of heteroglossia (the plurality of voices actually represented within a particular social context) will persist no matter how much the official discourse strives to make a monologue out of a dialogue.

We do not mean to suggest here that the official discourse that failed to control Ms. Jansen's class was entirely (or even primarily) created and maintained by her. While a teacher certainly has a significant degree of control over what goes on in the classroom, there are, of course, considerable constraints

Table 3.1. Student Literature Achievement and Class Behavior in Ms. Jansen's and Mr. Kramer's Classes

Class Achievement and Instructional Variables	Teacher	
	Ms. Jansen	Mr. Kramer
Achievement (Spring Literature Test score)	13.73	31.62
Proportion of teacher authentic questions	.70	.32
Proportion of students off task	.19	.04
Proportion of students active during question-answer recitation	.17	.96

on her that need to be acknowledged in a discussion of class activities. Primary among these constraints is a tracking system over which teachers often have no control (for a more general treatment of tracking, see Chapter 2). Ms. Jansen, for example, was working with "slightly below average" students who fell in the lower end of a four-track English curriculum; in our postobservational interview with her, she understandably voiced frustration with the constraints that the tracking system imposed on her. "[Some of my classes] have no positive role models in them," she told us. "It's really tough [to manage a class] when everyone needs extra help." This was especially true, according to Ms. Jansen, because the students *knew* that they were tracked. "They say things like, 'This is the dummy class.'" Yet, it was not only negative student attitudes that she was fighting against. "Before I got these students, I was told to lower my expectations." Ms. Jansen felt she was constantly fighting against the tracking system she had inherited. She insisted, for example, that students attempt to write whole essays about literature (like students in the higher tracks) rather than stopping at single paragraphs. We might understand the din that emerged to take over the class, then, as resistance to the monologism inherent in a tracking system in which students' agendas and abilities are assumed for them before they even meet the teacher. As some teachers pointed out to us, student stereotypes and perceptions of relationships between gender and authority also may play a role in classroom control at the secondary school level. They suggested that were a male teacher the head of this classroom, we might not have seen such visible resistance, regardless of students' attitudes toward the curriculum. Other teachers spoke to us about additional constraints that remained out of their hands to change — everything from the time of day a class met to distractions caused by special school events to PA announcements interrupting what might have been a "magical" turning point for a particular class.

Nonetheless, Ms. Jansen did help choose, at some level, the question-and-answer, quiz-and-review format that we observed. Given the comparatively poor overall performance of Ms. Jansen's students on a literature achievement exam designed to test knowledge of course texts (see Table 3.1), it seems that devoting class time to rote review is not necessarily an effective way to help students master texts — even in lower-track classes. It would seem that when literature teachers take a test-centered approach emphasizing recall of textual details, they send an implicit but powerful message to students that literature is not as important as literature tests. In effect, this emphasis on the product rather than the process of learning displaces the students from their roles in the production of knowledge. The students' alienation from the material is then reflected in their lack of investment in participation, if they participate at all.

We leave Ms. Jansen's class for a moment to investigate Mr. Kramer's classroom. Mr. Kramer's classroom puzzled us for exactly the opposite reason Ms. Jansen's did: Although he did not tend to ask authenic questions, his class performed far better than the students' prior performance and SES predicted. How did he as a teacher get students involved with material, if not primarily by engaging them with authentic questions?

CREATING A POSITIVE CLASSROOM CULTURE

Upon first listening to sessions of Mr. Kramer's ninth-grade literature classroom, it was hard to decide which impressed us more: the air of mutual respect pervading it, or the fact that he cultivated such an atmosphere without asking many authentic questions (or questions of any kind, for that matter). Mr. Kramer's opening comments to the 25 students in his class actually seemed to *discourage* teacher–student dialogue, especially when compared with Ms. Jansen's opening comments.

> What we're going to do is analyze a group of poems from the textbook. The way I analyze the poem is the way . . . I expect you to analyze the poems in the booklet. I'm not going to go through that many poetic devices, but I am going to analyze the poem in terms of themes, all right. The way I analyze the theme of the poem and the mood is the way I expect your analysis to be in the booklet. So what we can call these are simply dry runs, [to] sharpen your senses in terms of how you're going to do the booklet poems.

Mr. Kramer opened his literature class by dictating to the students exactly what he expected. Although ostensibly monologic, his opening, in contrast to Ms. Jansen's, shows that his greatest concern is being directive about the boundaries of *class activities and goals* — not about the boundaries separating "most important" answers from less important ones. The goal of his class appeared to be learning a certain methodology of analysis, whereas the goal of Ms. Jansen's class seemed to be reproducing her idea of right answers for multiple-choice tests.

These two goals were governed by radically divergent epistemologies. Mr. Kramer was striving to make his students *producers* of knowledge, while Ms. Jansen seemed to be creating *reproducers* of knowledge, despite the fact that her class goals included encouraging students to become critical readers. Given the overall epistemological goal that Mr. Kramer had, then, even a highly directive activity like modeling could be carried out in such a way as to value student input. Because student input ultimately counted, his directiveness regarding his expectations ("The way I analyze the poem is the way . . . I expect you to analyze the poems") opened the way for a more authentic teacher–student dialogue than the other teacher's assertion that "there are a lot of right answers."

Mr. Kramer's pedagogical practice could be seen as a kind of scaffolding. He suggested in the way he set up his class that control would be given over to the students bit by bit; students eventually would be responsible for conducting the activity of literature analysis on their own, but not before they had had some practice, or gone through some "dry runs," as he put it. The classroom dialogue we heard was often a group version of such dry runs. Mr. Kramer presented the methodology of analysis as a kind of dialogue with the text — in the following case, a poem about the relationship between a brother and sister struggling to survive during the Great Depression:

> MR. KRAMER: Now what about the final stanza? . . . . Look at the final stanza.
> STUDENT 1 (interrupts): She's showing that she's not as sure of everything as she says she is.
> MR. KRAMER (jumping in to read a segment of the poem): "He sees her . . ."
> STUDENT 2: Does that mean that she is nervous and trying to hide her feelings? She doesn't want him to think she's nervous.
> MR. KRAMER: Yeah, she's successfully hid her feelings, until like the neon sign that continually beats . . . the sign corresponds to what?
> Student: (inaudible)
> MR. KRAMER: Yeah, the beating of her veins, the vein pitifully beating almost like the sign continues to go . . . .

In this class segment, Mr. Kramer's open-ended question asking for interpretation of a poem ("Now what about the final stanza?") stands in contrast to Ms. Jansen's request for one-word, fill-in-the-blank answers. So does the ensuing pattern of dialogue. Although similar to the dialogue in Ms. Jansen's class, in that it was characterized by interruptions, the interruption noted above—a student interrupting Mr. Kramer to offer her reading of that stanza—was a sign of dialogic engagement rather than a shutting down of dialogue. Significantly, Mr. Kramer did not pause to evaluate her response; rather, he responded to her by reading a line from the last stanza that was the basis for her answer in the first place, thereby stimulating further conversation. Thus, by echoing the lines the student had focused on, Mr. Kramer affirmed the student's interpretation, rather than closing it down with a quick evaluation. This response also served to keep the text itself before the students so that others could jump in with their observations. Mr. Kramer's recurrent "yeah" was an ambiguous response, not a value judgment—communication whose purpose was simply to keep conversation going.

The conversation did keep going. An amazing 96% of Mr. Kramer's students participated constructively during the class session, in contrast to only 17% of Ms. Jansen's students (see Table 3.1).

THE SOCIAL LOGIC OF RECIPROCITY

Mr. Kramer's comments foregrounded the text as a "thinking device" (Lotman, 1988). The text in his class was not a univocal, static entity containing "the answers," but a tool to encourage students to reflect critically. As he echoed it and kept it in front of students, the text was given a voice. As Purves (1991) notes, "Once written, texts become alive only when they are read, and they become literary when a reader chooses to read them as aesthetic objects rather than as documents" (p. 161). Mr. Kramer read the words of the text with a dramatic flair that never allowed students to see it as a mere document. Furthermore, by stepping into the role of the text itself, he animated the poem, making explicit for his students the dialogic experience that is always a part of reading. In the above conversation, Mr. Kramer at once interrupted and refused to interrupt; he jumped into dialogue with the student, but assumed the role of the text in dialogue with her, rather than the role of the teacher. He encouraged her to interact with the text as aesthetic object rather than with himself as evaluator.

Thus we see the social logic of reciprocity at work: The role that the teacher assumes determines the role the students will assume (see Chapter 1). By assuming the role of the text, Mr. Kramer allowed students in the class to step into the role of reader rather than the role of student. Although it is impossible to tell whether the student in Mr. Kramer's class was responding more directly to the text or to her fellow student when she said, "Does that mean she is nervous and trying to hide her feelings?" it does not matter; response here builds upon response, leading to new knowledge rather than a list of right answers on the board. A dialogic approach to instruction encourages role shifting because it creates fluid boundaries between student, teacher, and text.

Purves's (1991) distinction between texts read as aesthetic objects and texts read as documents is a useful one to keep in mind when comparing Mr. Kramer's use of the text with Ms. Jansen's. Ms. Jansen, too, encouraged close reading of the text, but her text was clearly text as document.

> Ms. Jansen: Okay, analyze the scene at dinner and explain why John has some of his anxieties. This should be somewhere in Chapter 7 or 8. Who needs a book? What page is it on?
> Student 1: Fifty-seven.
> Ms. Jansen: Okay, look on page 57 and we'll find out the territory. . . . Okay, it's under "eating peas." Okay, who'd like to read just that — 57 to near the bottom of 58 where there's a gap.
> Brenda: I will.
> Ms. Jansen: Okay, Brenda.
> (Brenda reads the passage.)
> Ms. Jansen: Okay. The question, then, was, "Analyze the scene at dinner and explain why John has some of his anxieties."

It is important to remember that while the teacher asked the students to "analyze" the material, she was asking this question in the context of a question-and-answer recitation session: Brenda's reading of the text is followed by a review of right answers as to "why John has some of his anxieties." In contrast to Mr. Kramer, who assumed the role of the text, Ms. Jansen assumed the role of a *test,* asking the kinds of questions a test would ask. As noted above, her students' entire encounter with the text was framed in the context of a test-taking experience. The text itself was treated as what Hynds (1991) calls "a *container* for *correct meaning,* rather than fertile ground for exploration and interpretation" (p. 119; emphasis in original). The students did not appear to be at liberty to interpret what was before them. The teacher ended the class, in fact, looking not only back to the last quiz but also forward to future quizzes. "So if you don't have these [answers] down, get them down," Ms. Jansen cautioned. "These make ideal multiple-choice questions." Students were encouraged to become engaged with the "test" they eventually would have to take rather than with the piece of literature they had just read.

Our research has led us to conclude that, on the whole, the teacher should urge students to consider not just the text as a source of knowledge, but also themselves, their classmates, and their teacher; questions based in personal knowledge and others' knowledge mimic the dynamics of conversation. Nevertheless, Mr. Kramer shows how even text-based questions — or, what is more surprising, even inauthentic questions — can foster a dialogic atmosphere if the text is used as a thinking device. Consider the following exchange about narrative points of view:

MR. KRAMER: What is the other kind of narrator?
STUDENT 1: Third-person narrator.
MR. KRAMER: Well, yeah, third-person narrator. And what is that called? Somebody's whispering the word.
STUDENT 2: Omniscient narrator.
MR. KRAMER: What do you mean by "omniscient"?
STUDENT 2: (Inaudible)
MR. KRAMER: Yeah, yeah, yeah, yeah. Right. You are like a puppeteer. You see, that's the beauty of writing. Because that's the only time I know of where you are God. You are God when you write as the third-person narrator.

Note how Mr. Kramer follows up what sounds like a test question ("What is the other kind of narrator?"): He asks, "What do you mean by omniscient [narrator]?" rather than, "What is an omniscient narrator?" He is asking for the student's definition rather than *the* definition. This request for elaboration is not an attempt to push the student toward the "right" answer, but an attempt to encourage the student to explore her own "interpretive horizons." His request for elaboration shows that he is concerned not only with whether the students can remember a particular term, but with whether they understand it. It is a mark of his commitment to honoring student input that even the definition of a literary term is open to discussion. Thus, Mr. Kramer has set the tone for what a question in his classroom is — part of the larger exploratory dialogue going on between student and teacher.

That Mr. Kramer valued such dialogue was verified during our postobservational interview with him. His ideal student? "Those who think for themselves." His ideal class? "When you get kids to ask questions and start [making connections between] what's going on in the world today and what's going on in their own lives." Ms. Jansen's answers to our questions about her ideal student/classroom situation revealed a subtle but important difference: "The best classes are the ones where students do all their work, are excited about what we're doing, know when to be quiet and when to talk." Although students' ability to think critically and ask intelligent questions clearly mattered to her — these were in fact two things she eventually mentioned that she wanted her students to learn — the off-task behavior in her lower-track classes seemed to keep her focused on getting students to be compliant rather than to engage in conversation about the material. The consequences of tracking, it appears, had affected her approach — as well as Mr. Kramer's. Mr. Kramer, who worked with "above average" students, admitted to us that he would change his approach if working with the lower-track students: "I like to be myself in the classroom and to treat students on my level, and there's no way you can do that with an average group. I'd have to play a role every day. I'd have to be a stern disciplinarian. I couldn't joke much. I couldn't use a lot of my own personal experiences in there."

It is how teachers negotiate this larger classroom context, then, that plays such a great role in determining how any given strategy will be received by the students. As we noted in our discussion of Ms. Jansen's class, "conversation" in the context of a recitation class doesn't fly; neither does a request for analysis. Similarly, "recitation" in the context of a truly conversational class loses its sting. Only by looking at the context of the entire class can we understand why a particular move succeeds or fails to engage students in dialogic instruction.

Ultimately, then, understanding how Ms. Jansen's ostensibly "authentic" class talk could be stifling and Mr. Kramer's seemingly "inauthentic" class talk could be invigorating required examining not just teacher talk or student talk per se, but the *interactions* between teachers and students. It is in the interactions between conversants that meaning lies. In these two classrooms it was the *context* of each class session, built by the interactions — the classroom culture the teachers established, by giving instructions, implicitly or explicitly setting goals for the class and generally leading by example — that determined the authenticity of the teacher's questions in students' eyes. An "authentic" teacher question would not necessarily foster student dialogue, if the teacher's rigid question-and-answer format suggested that interpretive student responses were not actually welcome. Conversely, an apparently inauthentic question posed during a two-way discussion about the meaning of a poem could become a stepping stone to discussion if the teacher was perceived to be genuinely interested in students' interpretations. Classroom culture also determined what kinds of questions students felt allowed to ask, or were willing to risk asking. These two classrooms demonstrate that it is difficult, if not impossible, to understand the full impact of teacher and student questions apart from the context of the class in which they occur.

Different Kinds of Classroom Control

Our tale of two classrooms finally brings us back to the question we posed at the beginning of this chapter: Are the conditions that determine whether a productive dialogue between teacher and student can take place within the teacher's control — and, if so, to what degree? We have come to believe that certain fundamental conditions *are* within the teacher's control.

First and foremost, teachers help determine the context in which classroom talk happens — the classroom's format and its underlying epistemology. It is the teacher who determines how classroom talk will be structured, whether as a lecture, question-and-answer session, or discussion. It is the teacher who decides whether simply to pass along knowledge to students or to use students' input to start discussions that allow new knowledge to be generated.

The discourse in Ms. Jansen's and Mr. Kramer's classrooms illustrates two different kinds of teacher control. Both teachers obviously sought some kind of control over their classrooms — hoping, no doubt, to make sure that learning happened. The critical difference between their attempts to exert authority in the classroom is this: *while Ms. Jansen's discourse limited the actual knowledge produced in her classroom, Mr. Kramer's discourse controlled the process students went through in generating knowledge.* Ms. Jansen looked for right answers, while Mr. Kramer concerned himself with whether students arrived at answers in the right way, and whether he and they were creating an environment conducive to learning.

The notion that there is a positive kind of control apart from the kind that silences student dialogue, is an important one. Too often, teachers shy away from attempts to share control of the classroom with students because they fear the prospect of relinquishing all authority; they recognize all too well the "power of peer dynamics to . . . subvert . . . educational goals" (DiPardo & Freedman, 1988, p. 127). The felt need to adopt an all-or-nothing attitude toward taking control of the classroom, however, is a misperception. Teachers must channel their authority productively by choosing to exert the kind of control that stimulates learning.

Culture Building in the Classroom: Yalom's Theory

Irvin D. Yalom (1995), a clinical psychologist and theorist of group dynamics, makes helpful distinctions between different kinds of control that a leader can take. Drawing on his many years of experience as a facilitator in peer-centered, group therapy settings, he argues that leaders who believe that learning lies in facilitating peer interaction must exert their authority, but only in very specific ways. First, leaders of groups must proactively introduce people to the new culture they will experience in the group. He calls this "culture building." Culture building involves establishing "a code of behavioral rules, or norms, . . . that will guide the interaction of the group" (p. 109). It is important to make clear to the students that each class, like other groups who convene for special purposes, "has norms that radically depart from the rules, or etiquette, of typical social intercourse" (p. 110). Yalom lists a number of norms that are important to establish in groups where peer interaction is emphasized. We believe that many, if not all, of the group norms that follow would enhance classroom experience if modeled by teachers and embraced by students:

- Expression is honest and spontaneous.
- Interaction between members is free.
- Levels of personal involvement are high.
- Members desire insight and change.
- Self-disclosure is safe and highly valued.
- Members take responsibility for the group's effectiveness.
- Members consider the group important.
- Communicating about material of relevance to the group as a whole takes priority over discussing outside material.
- Members consider each other their primary agents of help.

According to Yalom, the peer-centered leader should construct these norms explicitly, acting as the group's "technical expert." This is exactly what Mr. Kramer did at the beginning of his class. As mentioned above, he began a classroom segment on interpreting poetry by clearly laying out the methodological guidelines that he expected students to follow: "The way I analyze the poem is the way . . . I expect you to analyze the poems in the booklet." Furthermore, just before beginning that poetry segment, he spent several minutes outlining his expectations for work due in the coming week. The phrase "I want," in fact, was repeated five times in less than 2 minutes! He was setting parameters for what was expected of these people when they got together. In contrast, Ms. Jansen does not seem to invest much time in laying out parameters for the group task at hand: "Okay, we're going to go over yesterday's study guide from the quiz. . . . We should come up with a bunch of different things." Perhaps, too, the "task at hand" is so woefully familiar in this case that students need not be informed anew of the role they will play.

We also noticed in Ms. Jansen's classroom a seeming absence of group maintenance, Yalom's second essential component to culture building. Group maintenance includes deterring "any forces that threaten group cohesiveness[:] Continued tardiness, absences, subgrouping, disruptive extragroup socialization, and scapegoating" (Yalom, 1995 p. 107). Even if it means removing an individual from a group, the leader's "first task is to help create a physical entity, a group" (p. 107). Although Ms. Jansen reported spending a significant amount of time on "classroom management," she tended to ignore disruptions in the classes we observed; the high incidence of off-task chatter that continued as a result suggested that class activity was not generally valued. As a relatively new teacher, she was, understandably, still struggling to find appropriate ways to exert her authority in the class: "I never thought when I was student teaching that discipline would be such an issue or problem," she told us. "It is probably what I was least prepared for."

Yalom's framework helped us identify another potential problem in Ms. Jansen's classroom: a tendency to hastily evaluate student responses, which did not leave space for any kind of productive exchange to develop. Yalom calls this jumping into "content commentary" too soon. A leader who does this hinders her group's dialogic potential by sending the message that knowledge flows in only one direction — a message that students are prone to internalize quickly, given the very real institutional authority with which teachers are invested. Only the teacher or group leader who proactively decenters her voice in the early weeks of a class by focusing on culture building and group maintenance activities can, according to Yalom, earn the right to make evaluative commentary without setting herself up as the authority who "owns" the knowledge produced in the classroom. Mr. Kramer proactively decentered his voice this way when he chose to play the role of the text rather than the role of the evaluator in the illustrative class segment above, thus allowing student voices to occupy center stage. In addition, his language expressed an excitement and intensity that reinforced the classroom culture he had created; it suggested that the most important exchange of ideas was happening front and center rather than on the fringes of the class. By himself maintaining a respect for the process of learning and the input of his students, Mr. Kramer encouraged his students to respect the learning situation as well. He helped ensure that the classroom would be a safe place for productive, honest exchange.

BEYOND THE NEXT TEST

As we suggested earlier, the fact that Mr. Kramer created a classroom culture in which students felt ownership of their ideas allowed him, without violating their trust, to ask questions with prespecified answers. In a class where dialogism is an ingrained value, the knowledge that the teacher brings to the class can encourage a sense of security rather than a feeling of passive detachment. The students in Mr. Kramer's class who were asked about the meaning of "omniscient narrator" so that they ultimately could use that concept to do their own thinking about literature, for example, did not share the same classroom experience as the students in Ms. Jansen's class who were quizzed paragraph by paragraph on the one right meaning of the short story they read. In Socratic fashion, Mr. Kramer asked questions that were worth thinking about, even if they did have prespecified answers. They were worth thinking about because they carried implications beyond the classroom.

More important, students were being asked to consider things that might be useful even after the next test. What was striking about Mr. Kramer's class was not his commitment to asking students questions, however, but his commitment to fostering what Tharp and Gallimore (1988) call "instructional conversation."[2] Perhaps the rarity of student questions in the class should not surprise us; real-life conversation typically is not dominated by questions.

The bottom line in dialogic instruction, then, is not any one "do" or "don't" — asking open-ended questions, setting up discussion formats, or totally eschewing lectures and review sessions. As Langer and Applebee (1987) point out in their study of process approaches to writing, piecemeal changes in pedagogical practice are rarely effective if unaccompanied by a basic reconceptualization of overall goals and expectations. With regard to student engagement, what matters most is taking students' input seriously, so that a context for the kind of dialogue that leads to learning can take place even in situations that might seem univocal, as in a class dominated by lecture. As in any context, good conversation happens when mutual trust and respect exist between the parties conversing, and when both parties believe that something new can be discovered by talking things out. Without this ethos of mutual respect, the classroom atmosphere will tend toward monologism, no matter who is actually doing the talking.

CHAPTER 4

What's a Teacher to Do?
Dialogism in the Classroom

Martin Nystrand

THE KIND OF INSTRUCTION supported by the results of this study will seem utopian and impractical to many. Fully dialogic instruction, first of all, involves a conception of knowledge not as previously formulated by someone else but rather as continuously regenerated and co-constructed among teachers and learners and their peers. In addition, dialogic instruction eschews recitation and the one-way transmission of information from teacher to students—far and away the predominant form of classroom discourse in American schools today—in favor of a seemingly vague process of "negotiating meanings" and "transforming understandings" in open-ended discussion and instructional "conversation." Such exchanges require that teachers abandon the security of their roles as authoritative repositories and referees of unproblematic knowledge in favor of the more subtle and ostensibly risky roles of master conversant, catalyst, critic, and organizer of dialogue. Dialogic methods put a premium on close teacher–student interaction, a high degree of individualization, peer groups, open-ended discussion, and curricula and lesson plans that are not completely planned in advance. Lessons are expected to unfold partly in response to student contributions and a sequence of classroom interactions that cannot be entirely predicted. Above all, dialogic instruction depends for its success on what students bring to class. Yet for many educators, parents, taxpayers, and pundits, American students seem distinguished above all by what they *fail* to bring to class. Can such a proposal possibly work? Education policy makers seem bent on a national curriculum and increased testing. They will wonder how teachers and schools can possibly be accountable if they leave anything more to chance than they already do.

CURRENTLY USED DIALOGIC METHODS

Many teachers currently use a variety of methods that officially accommodate and nurture the inherent dialogicality of their classrooms to promote learning and achievement. Indeed, our study uncovered several methods consistent with these principles, including *uptake, authentic questions, and high-level evaluation*. Regrettably, however, few teachers use them all consistently. As we have seen, by incorporating previous student answers into subsequent questions, many teachers use uptake to follow up and elaborate student perceptions and interpretations. By asking authentic questions and not prespecifying answers, teachers open the floor to student interpretations, signaling to students that *their* ideas — and not just those presented in their textbooks — are important and can provide opportunities for learning. Finally, through high-level evaluation, teachers ratify the importance of student responses, allowing their ideas and observations to affect the course of the discussion in substantive ways. Teachers practicing these methods establish ground rules for classroom discourse that validate student response by accommodating information that moves from students to teacher and back, not just from teacher to students.

Classroom Conversations: Shared Negotiations of Meaning

Many effective teachers continuously interrelate writing, reading, and classroom talk. In these classrooms, students talk about topics before writing about them, and then write about what they discuss; they write about what they have read; they discuss what they have written, and follow up their discussions with reading. A successful class discussion, over the course of a given lesson, builds an intricate network of understandings as each piece of new information sequentially transforms and expands given information into new understandings. For example, in the discussion of *Roll of Thunder, Hear My Cry* (see Chapter 1), the fourth chapter of the novel could be treated as a source of given information since students had written plot summaries for it as homework the previous night. In the segment presented in Chapter 1, the student, John, highlighted some of this given information when he noted that Mr. Turner "resisted white help." The teacher then asked why he did this, and John replied by introducing new information (i.e., new to this discussion) that Turner continued to shop at the store because "all the others were white." This conjecture turned out to be wrong, however, so John revised his hypothesis, elaborating additional new information: "Here's the reason," he claimed: "They don't get paid till the cotton comes in. But throughout the year they still have to buy stuff. . . . So the owner of the plantation will sign for what they buy at the store so that throughout the year they can still buy stuff on credit."

This excerpt can be viewed as a *sequence of dynamically co-constructed understandings,* each building on a previous one while anticipating the next. Discourse typically is distinguished by such "chains" of given and new information so that the succession of one response to another defines the tempo of the talk. The final understanding of any discussion — sometimes called the gist — consequently reflects a unique history of dynamic interactions of particular conversants. After some particularly "hot" classroom discussions, teachers are sometimes frustrated when they fail to repeat the same discussion with the next class, which, unfortunately, proceeds to elaborate the same topic quite differently. The reason is simple: Each discussion has its own life, and different conversants will always interact differently.

For Britton (1969), this sort of language, whether written or spoken, is *expressive*. In his analysis of student talk about a Hemingway short story, he writes:

> The language remains "expressive" throughout, in the sense that it is relaxed, self-presenting, self-revealing, addressed to a few intimate companions; in the sense that it moves easily from general comment to narration of particular experiences and back again; and in the special sense that in making comments the speakers do not aim at accurate, explicit reference (as one might in an argument or sociological report) and in relating experience they do not aim at a polished performance (as a raconteur or a novelist would). (1969, p. 96)

This sort of discourse is pedagogically important, Britton goes on to point out, because in the process of talking, the students work through just those concepts that need to be internalized, precisely in terms of what they already know. Such discussion is noteworthy not as a report of what has been assigned but rather for its potential as a mode of learning itself.

In dialogic terms, given information is what the conversants know together, whereas new information is what is *not* shared by the conversants in a given situation. That is, newness and givenness are always relative to who is talking.

The process of negotiating new understandings involves orienting individuals in fundamental epistemological ways, not just denoting and reciting concepts (Becker, 1992b, p. 119). As we have seen, monologic genres of classroom discourse such as recitation and study questions tend to elicit reports of information. By contrast, dialogic genres such as authentic questions, discussion, and sustained position papers tend to elicit analysis and interpretation. When teachers respond to students by evaluating their answers, as in the common IRE sequence of recitation (i.e., teacher Initiation–student Response–teacher Evaluation), they treat learning as remembering and students as rememberers. By contrast, when teachers respond to students by making an observation of their own, as in conversation and discussion, they treat learning as reflection and validate students not just as rememberers but also as thinkers. In effect, these different genres of discourse assign or impute fundamentally different roles to students, and thus they entail an ethical choice by the teacher. As Maturana and Varela explain, the "linkage of human to human is, in the final analysis, the groundwork of all ethics as a reflection on the legitimacy of the presence of others" (cited in Becker, 1992a, p. 231). In taking students seriously, teachers elicit the best from students by expecting the most. If teachers nurse the full potential of each classroom discussion, they will resist prescripted, "canned" interactions and constantly be ready to respond thoughtfully to the unique responses of each class.

Certain kinds of classroom talk and writing assignments, such as journals, drafts, and learning logs, afford far more opportunity and flexibility than others, such as study questions and tests, for contextualizing and assimilating new information. In writing a draft or keeping a learning log, the writer and reader are one and the same, whereas in more typical writing tasks the writer and reader are not the same. This difference affects the given and new information that the writer must balance. In an exam situation, the student must discuss new concepts in terms of whatever the teacher assumes to be given, presumably previous course content. In the learning log, by contrast, students have an opportunity more fully to appropriate new concepts because they may deal with them not only in terms of previous course content, but also in terms of anything else that might seem relevant. In an eleventh-grade learning log in English, for example, a student may write tentatively, "I'm not sure what caused Macbeth's downfall. It was his ambition. But it was also Lady Macbeth's ambition. What did the witches have to do with it?" The writer may also digress: "Maybe if I went back and looked at the soliloquies, this might make more sense. Let's see. . . ." In addition, students may write in logs tentatively and speculatively about course readings. Such entries could never be submitted, however, as exam answers: The "tentativeness" would be judged as a sign of "uncertainty," and the digressions would be viewed as a sign of "incoherence." Neither would be allowed, let alone encouraged, in an exam-driven curriculum, despite their importance to the learner's engagement with the subject.

What dialogism adds to our understanding of instruction concerns the way in which students' interactions with their teachers and peers provide a social foundation for learning. As we have seen, promoting conceptual change in dialogic terms involves interacting with and responding to others. These conversations may take written form, of course; what counts is that the conversants seek to engage each other on their own terms. That is, conceptual change occurs not when teachers "transmit" new information to students but rather when different voices or perspectives "interpenetrate" and "interanimate" each other in such a way that the interpretive frameworks of the conversants are modified and expanded in the process. Effective teachers commonly do this by starting on familiar ground and encouraging students to draw on their prior knowledge, current understandings, and personal experience as they grapple with new material. Authentic questions, uptake, and discussion can all serve this purpose. Good teachers continuously reflect on "where we are now" in order to understand "where we can go next."

Epistemologically, dialogically organized instruction treats present-tense, constructive, and sometimes tentative knowing—that is, the learner's current understanding—as the foundation of past-tense knowledge (what gets remembered) and therefore learning. To accommodate the multiple voices of dialogic classrooms, teachers must do more than present information, and students must do more than find out and remember what someone else knows. Students must not merely master other people's ideas and facts collected by others for later recall. Rather, learning requires them to integrate new information into their current understanding of the world and their experience. For this reason, effective instruction makes room for the evolution of students' understandings as well as the new information they must learn, as Ms. Lindsay's class did for John (see Chapter 1).

Every word has a multitude of potential meanings, and precisely the one or ones realized in discourse, Rommetveit (1983) argues, will depend on "what at the moment of utterance is taken for granted by both conversation partners" (p. 18).[1] For example, in teaching modern French history in a culture where the concept of "president" is utterly meaningless (Rommetveit chooses rural Africa as an example), a teacher may explain this concept with a compromised yet functional reference to Charles de Gaulle as a "powerful king of France." Rommetveit (1974) explains:

> And the teacher's reason for employing that particular expression may be by no means malevolent or cynical: The fact may simply be that in that particular situation he can hit upon no better means of bridging the gap between what the students already know of relevance to the topic and what at such a stage of preknowledge can be made known to them about de Gaulle and his political role in France. (p. 34)

Even though the phrase "powerful king of France" is not a valid definition of president in a modern European democracy, it nonetheless communicates effectively in this situation.

"Understanding itself," Vološinov (1973) claims, "can come about only within some kind of semiotic material" (p. 11), such as classroom discourse. This is because meaning is a dynamic phenomenon coming about as multiple voices and differing points of view refract and respond to each other.[2] Understanding is promoted especially by conflict, disagreement, and struggle of contrasting perspectives. Understanding always takes the form of a response.

> To understand another's person utterance means to orient oneself with respect to it. . . . For each word of the utterance that we are in process of understanding,

we, as it were, lay down a set of our own answering words. . . . *Any true understanding is dialogic in nature.* Understanding is to utterance as one line of a dialogue is to the next. Understanding strives to match the speaker's work with a *counter word.* (Vološinov, 1973, p. 102; emphasis in original)

In the sense that events are said to be interpreted and not simply input to memory, the process of dialogic understanding is somewhat similar to cognitive psychologists' treatment of comprehension as the assimilation or contextualization of new information in terms of current understandings (cf. Piaget, 1951). Unlike cognitive psychologists, however, Vološinov and Bakhtin view understanding not in terms of abstract mental representations (schemata) but rather as the "refraction" of one sign by another. "Meaning," Vološinov asserts, "does not reside in the word or in the soul of the speaker or in the soul of the listener. Meaning is the *effect of interaction between speaker and listener.* . . . It is like an electric spark that occurs only when two different terminals are hooked together" (Vološinov, 1973, pp. 102–103; emphasis in original); a given utterance is "understood against the background of other concrete utterances on the same theme, a background made up of contradictory opinions, points of view and value judgments" (Bakhtin, 1981, p. 281). It is just such a context that often is enhanced in dialogically organized instruction by position papers on engaging subjects and by journal writing and authentic teacher questions, all of which favor heteroglossia because they invite student voices into the unfolding discourse of class. These activities foster instructional contexts in which students may, as Vološinov (1973) writes, "give [themselves] verbal shape from another's point of view" (p. 86).

Reciprocity in the Zone of Proximal Development

Vygotsky, a contemporary of Bakhtin and Vološinov (though he apparently never met them), conceptualized learning and cognitive development as just such a dialogic play of consciousness between learners and teachers, including more able peers. According to Vygotsky, children largely experience language as interactions with parents and siblings; this interaction serves to coordinate their activity with each other. Indeed, young children even talk to themselves, particularly in the midst of complicated tasks, Vygotsky observes, as a way of regulating their own behavior. Self-regulation is possible, he claims, only after a period of interaction with adults and more capable peers. Their interaction is most likely to be successful, moreover, when it occurs in the *zone of proximal development:* "the distance between the actual developmental level . . . and the level of potential development" (Vygotsky, 1978, p. 86). Development occurs when "what a child can do with assistance today" becomes transformed into what "she will be able to do by herself tomorrow" (p. 87).

All this is by now, of course, common knowledge among literacy researchers. What is not always appreciated, however, is how sequences of well-scaffolded interactions (Bruner, 1978) between adults and children are based on a reciprocity of roles rooted in some common activity, for example, game playing. Wertsch and Hickmann (1987) elucidate this aspect of development in a study of mothers teaching their children to draw pictures of trucks. The mothers begin by showing the children how to draw, making all or most of the lines themselves, and then, in subsequent interactions, they gradually make fewer lines and shapes as the children learn (internalize) the procedures. Hence, in a coordinating effort, the adult "scaffolds" the learning and activity of the child, Wertsch (1979, 1985) points out, by allowing for what the child can do (actual developmental level) while providing support for what the child is not yet able to do (potential developmental level). Continually honoring the expanding role and perspective and the emerging skills of the child, the adult gradually allows the child to assume more responsibility for the task as her potential skills are transformed into actual ones. In dialogic terms — and this is the essential point — each performs according to the demands of the social logic of their relationship. This logic not only configures their relationship while the child is learning but, as it becomes embedded in cognition, continues to organize the child's thinking and mature interactions once learning has happened. Development is understood here as the child's expanding role reciprocally entailed and hence enabled by the adult's receding role in a joint activity; roles can shift precisely because reciprocity remains constant. As Cazden (1988) points out, the key to scaffolding is the temporary and flexible nature of the supports. Such instruction is socially interactive because of its collaborative nature and because the adult must determine the nature of the required supports by estimating the state of the child's understanding. In this way, discourse and social interaction structure the development of the child's understanding. This is why, Vološinov (1973) argued, learning can take place only "on interindividual territory" (p. 12) — that is, between a learner and a teacher, between a self and a pedagogical other.

Forman and Cazden (1985) and Daiute and Dalton (1989) have shown that, even in the absence of a knowledgeable adult, peer collaboration can engage students in their zones of proximal development when, in working together on tasks of mutual interest, for example, each conversant stretches to realize the potential of the joint project. Although most contemporary discussions of instructional scaffolding refer to adult guidance of children's problem solving, Vygotsky (1978) himself referred to "problem solving under adult guidance or *in collaboration with more capable peers*" (p. 86; emphasis added). In their study of the collaboration of third graders working in pairs to compose narratives, Daiute and Dalton (1989) found that expertise is relative. Some students provided support on such technical matters as spelling and punctuation, and others contributed ideas on narrative structure.

One use of scaffolding in elementary reading instruction is Palincsar and Brown's (1984) *reciprocal teaching,* in which teachers and students engage in a dialogue in which the participants take turns assuming the role of teacher. Initially, teachers give detailed instructions and provide modeling to show students how to adopt appropriate roles. As the students gain proficiency, the teachers play an increasingly more passive role.

Langer and Applebee (1984) conclude that properly scaffolded instruction in English and language arts allows students to develop a sense of ownership in their work because they are able to "develop their own meaning rather than simply following the dictates of the teacher or text" (p. 180). Carefully scaffolded tasks, they contend, are sufficiently difficult to challenge but not so difficult as to frustrate students. Finally, they add that teachers are more likely to be effective when their role is collaborative rather than evaluative. Such collaborative interaction is possible in writing instruction, they contend, only when writing tasks encompass the students' as well as the teacher's purposes.

WRITING INSTRUCTION

The problem of learning to write in school is a little like learning a sport (e.g., tennis) entirely with coaching and no actual play. It is all well and good for an expert instructor to teach the fine points of proper strokes and strategy and to make observations from the sidelines, but unless this instruction is supplemented by actual interactions with a real player on the other side of the net, it is likely to remain abstract, hypothetical, and unrealized.

Unfortunately, students learning to write in school hear too many fine points about the features of proper texts, without much opportunity to write in an actual rhetorical context, that is, with very many readers "on the other side" of their texts. First, students tend to write mainly in English class and not much in other subjects, despite recent National Assessment of Educational Progress results showing that students are writing somewhat more in other subjects (see, e.g., Applebee et al., 1994). Furthermore, because of large classes and student loads, most English teachers assign relatively few pieces of writing. Finally, teachers tend to provide expert feedback on text features and technical matters, not rhetorical purpose, in response to instructional tasks Britton and colleagues (1975) call "dummy runs," and what Burgess (1985) describes as not "real and continuous writing at all, but routine, unreal and mystifying — a busywork succession of trivial exercises" (p. 54).

When teachers do respond to the writer's rhetorical purpose, they do so as coach, not actual reader. Imagine a student writer's surprise (not to mention that of her parents and her teacher's principal) if she were to receive a failing grade for an essay supporting abortion because, the teacher said, she had failed to change his mind; he still opposed abortion!

Teachers are expected to offer advice based on the response of an abstract individual that students never meet — "the reader." Although students receive advice and assessments concerning their texts, they rarely have the opportunity in school to change someone's mind or explain something their teacher does not already understand or know about. While such writing may help students to practice spelling and punctuation and recall essential course information, it unfortunately gives them little if any real experience in writing persuasive or informative prose — the teacher does not read their papers to be either persuaded or informed. Applebee (1981) comments:

> For learning to write well, the most effective writing situation will be one in which the effectiveness of the writing matters — where the student can savor the success of having presented a convincing argument or struggle with the problems of having failed to do so. In such situations the teacher can sometimes intervene directly, helping students develop their writing skills by demonstrating the effects of different methods of organization and presentation. If all that really matters, however, is that the right items of information can be cited, then the development of such new writing skills will be essentially irrelevant, and they will ignored by student and teacher alike. (p. 101)

Effective writing instruction requires practice and feedback in authentic rhetorical situations, where readers respond to the writer's actual purpose.

Perhaps the most important insight from recent research on composition is that effective writing instruction is less a matter of teaching knowledge *about* composition, rhetoric, or grammar, and more a matter of promoting and refining the process of writing by helping students know *how to proceed*. English teachers need to think of writing as a verb, not as a noun. In any case, information about writing (e.g., parts of speech, principles of rhetoric, types of paragraphs, etc.) makes the best sense to students in the context of the activity itself. This is why writing teachers' primary responsibility concerns initiating and sustaining appropriate writing activities and arranging for effective feedback, particularly in response groups and writing conferences.

How do skilled writers proceed? In school, we expect students to write well-developed, clear, explicit prose. As we saw in Chapter 1, however, this is never really a matter of *saying everything*. Rather, it requires being "attuned to the attunement of the other" (Rommetveit, 1992) — anticipating readers' "responsive understandings" (Bakhtin, 1986) and perspectives, and responding to the differences. At "choice points," skilled writers provide essential definitions and helpful examples. When their texts are then read, readers intuitively sense that the writer has lucidly spelled out *everything,* but in reality the writer has done no such thing; rather she has elaborated only potential threats to reciprocity—those points that, if left unelaborated, would be unclear and raise questions. Conversely, difficult texts either fail to treat such points or elaborate them in ways that make matters worse.[3] This is why explicitness is not a text phenomenon at all but rather a dialogic one and why, generally, discourse is so completely structured by the interactions of the conversants (Nystrand & Wiemelt, 1991). This is also why experience with a variety of reader response—more than just one or two teachers a year—is of great benefit to students learning to write.

If writing is a process of elaborating one's ideas in a comprehensible and effective manner, then learning to write requires gaining control over this process. What governs the choices and elaborations that writers make? According to Flower and Hayes (1977), these decisions are made by a "monitor" (i.e., the cognitive faculty that coordinates writing processes), yet just what makes this "black-box" tick? Just how does it decide when to plan, when to evaluate, when to transcribe, and when to revise? Why do basic writers miss essential choice points? In short, how are skilled writing processes structured? How can teachers use insights into these processes to define useful tasks and classroom contexts that help students identify appropriate choice points and generate useful elaborations? If we can define these choice points, we can go a long way toward addressing essential issues such as these. If our students can learn to anticipate salient choice points in their own writing and effectively treat them, their writing will improve.

To address these issues, writing researchers recently have focused on the relationship of the writing process to both its product, the text, and the contexts in which it operates. Specifically, they have examined the role that written texts play in mediating the needs of the writer for expression, on the one hand, and the reader for comprehension, on the other. Peer-response groups, in which students present their writing to classmates for discussion and feedback, constitute a critical pedagogical forum in which this process is enacted. In such groups, student authors have the opportunity to learn how their writing works to "bridge" their own purposes as authors with the concerns of readers. In dialogic terms, "[Message] X is not transmitted from [the writer] to the [reader], but is constructed between them as a kind of ideological bridge, is built in the process of their interaction" (Bakhtin/Medvedev, 1985, p. 152). Along these lines, Tierney and LaZansky (1980) postulate a writer–reader contract that "defines what is allowable *vis-à-vis* the role of each in relation to the text" (p. 2). Instruction is therefore helpful when students gain control over those elements of text that Brandt (1990) calls "metadiscoursal"—words and phrases like *however, moreover, on the other hand,* and so forth—that guide readers' reading and facilitate writers' interactions with them. Good instruction also helps students anticipate and therefore facilitate reader response, for example, by elaborating difficult terms with familiar examples or definitions. If students are to gain mastery of these processes, they need more than technical information (i.e., concerning grammar and usage) about the features of good texts. Above all, they need practice with and feedback from a wide range of readers, certainly more than teachers.

There are several ways that teachers can give their students experience with writing as a communicative process. The key to all of them is establishing audiences for their students that transcend teachers. For example, in addition to responding themselves to their students' writing, many teachers ask students to try their texts out with each other, and provide classtime for such draft swapping. Some high school English teachers establish class newspapers and magazines in which they "publish" their students' writing. Other teachers arrange for their students to be pen pals with students in other schools. Some teachers, in schools with networked computers, provide for peer writing using microcomputers (Huston & Thompson, 1985).

Peer-Response Groups in the Writing Classroom

Perhaps the most easily available audience for student writers is that made up by peers. Considerable research has demonstrated the effectiveness of peer conferencing, in which groups of four or five students regularly meet in class to present their papers for discussion with each other. In writing about elementary and high school English teaching, Moffett (1968) originally justified peer conferencing on the grounds that it was "the only way, short of tutorial, to provide individual students enough experience and feedback" (p. 12; see also Heath & Branscombe, 1985). Daiute (1986, 1989; Daiute & Dalton, 1993) shows that children as young as 8 benefit from collaborative writing, especially if it promotes the self-evaluation and justification of their ideas. The regular use of writing groups is a seminal idea for cutting down the paper load of high school English teachers who regularly must deal with 150 students or more and still want their students to write regularly. In some of these classrooms, students respond to most of the drafts that their peers write and then submit to the teacher a portfolio of only the best, finished pieces.

There are other important benefits associated with response groups. Research on peer conferencing, including studies of high school students, has demonstrated its effectiveness in contributing to gains in critical thinking, organization, and appropriateness (Lagana, 1973); revision skills (Benson, 1979; Nystrand & Brandt, 1989); attention to prewriting; awareness of writers' own writing processes (Nystrand, 1983); the ability to evaluate the likely success of writers' own texts (Nystrand & Brandt, 1989); and increased writer

confidence (Fox, 1980). For a review of this research, see DiPardo and Freedman (1988). In studies of peer conferencing, benefits were found for students
writing mainly for each other in small groups as compared with students who
wrote only for the teacher and spent no time in groups (Nystrand, 1986;
Nystrand & Brandt, 1989). These studies found that the writing ability of
first-year college students who regularly discussed their papers with peers improved more over the course of a semester than that of their counterparts
who wrote only for the teacher. The peer-group students' progress was due
mainly to the development of superior revising skills. One reason for this was
that the students simply did more revising; on average they revised each paper
about three times. In addition, as they presented their papers orally to their
groups, they developed proofreading skills and typically marked up their papers even before starting group discussion. The significance of this extensive
revising and proofreading went beyond its frequency, however, since these
activities were undertaken not as obligatory steps in a prescribed sequence of
composing behaviors but rather in the interest of making their texts functional for the members of their group; that is, their revisions were situation-
ally motivated.

Students who wrote mainly for each other in these studies usefully addressed discrepancies between what they meant and what their texts actually
said. By contrast, students who wrote only for their teacher treated problems
more as discrepancies between their text and some "ideal" text (Gere & Stevens, 1985). Over the course of the semester, the peer-group students increasingly viewed revision as a global process of reconceptualizing (rethinking the
purpose and development of their papers), whereas the teacher-only students
increasingly saw revision as a matter of tidying up their texts (mainly correct-
ing such "local" problems as typos, spelling, punctuation, and word choice).
This difference between the two groups related to the fact that students writing just for their teacher increasingly saw the teacher/reader as a "judge" of
their work, whereas students writing mainly for each other came to see their
peer readers as collaborators and helpers. Students in peer groups developed
more positive attitudes toward writing. This does not mean that the peer-
group students dealt less with errors and other writing problems; on the con-
trary, they were more openly critical of their own writing than were the
teacher-only writers. Response-group students, moreover, were able to relate
their revisions more accurately and explicitly to actual readers' needs, not simply to the needs of an anonymous, reified reader ("the Reader"). They more
adequately tailored their revisions to specific rhetorical problems and developed a more functional approach to writing and revising.

In another study demonstrating the pedagogical usefulness of peer response, Cohen and Riel (1989) compared the papers students wrote for their
teachers with those they wrote on the same topics for peers in another country

via a computer network. The papers addressed to peers were judged consistently to be of significantly higher quality than those written for the teachers, even though the students knew the papers for their teachers would figure prominently in their final grades. The peer papers were better in content, organization, vocabulary, language use, and mechanics. Cohen and Riel (1989) concluded that students write best in functional writing environments where, instead of writing to practice and demonstrate their skill to a teacher, they write to explain something to readers needing to know.

In an ethnographic study of nine elementary school Latino children, Gutierrez (1993) found that writing developed best to the extent that the students had opportunities to "elaborate on their own and others' responses, to ask critical questions, and to assume the multiple roles of reader, writer, and critic" (p. 15).

All these studies address a central difficulty of learning to write in school, namely, that students rarely get the chance to explain anything to someone who really needs or wants to know. As Applebee (1982) observes, writing for teachers is complicated because the teachers' knowledge usually circumscribes that of the students. Consequently, when students write for teachers, they address someone who reads not to be informed but rather to assess the state of the students' knowledge and skills. As Berkenkotter (1981) concludes, "School writing stifles the development of audience representation because it precludes its necessity" (p. 396).

Collaborative Learning and Other Small-Group Work

Response groups are, of course, only one instructional use for small groups and belong to a general category of instruction called collaborative learning. The benefits of this work include individualizing instruction, raising the perceived value of academic achievement, and improving race relations (Stallings & Stipek, 1986).

Research on small groups in literature classes also highlights instructional contexts that promote conceptual change. For example, in an empirical study of various modes of instruction on writing about nonfiction, Sweigart (1991) found that student-led, small-group discussions of nonfiction were superior to both lecture and whole-class discussion in helping students recall and understand essays they read. The small-group discussions he studied were also superior in preparing students to write analytic, opinion essays, which were scored for clear thesis and elaboration of ideas. In a study of the effectiveness of small groups in ninth-grade literature instruction, we found that small groups can be effective, but only if students are allowed some degree of autonomy to work out their own interpretations in response to open-ended tasks (Nystrand, Gamoran, & Heck, 1992; see also Chapter 2, this volume). Conversely, we found that when teachers organize small-group work around such tightly structured activities as collaborating on worksheets, students' comprehension and recall actually suffer by comparison with the more dialogic groups. In the best small groups we observed, the teacher clearly defined the general task parameters — for example, asking students to determine character motives or find the most revealing descriptions — but avoided telling groups exactly how to proceed.

In a study of collaborative writing involving multiple authors composing single texts, Dale (1992) provides insights into the role that social context can play in conceptual change. Dale studied ninth graders who collaborated in groups of three to write position papers on whether schools should make birth control available to high school students. She found, first, that the strongest groupwork, which developed the most substantive ideas, was characterized by the most extensive cognitive conflict. This replicates the finding of Perret-Clermont (1980) that peer interaction promotes reasoning and cognitive reorganization when differing perspectives engender cognitive conflict. Dale also found that the talk of this group was especially coherent as students followed up on each other's points; this coherence was strikingly obvious in conversational tags in which students expanded and modified each other's sentences. By contrast, the weakest group was characterized by hostility and little discussion that went beyond only the most general of ideas — which resulted, curiously, in the weakest group spending far more time than the strongest group in explicitly representing the task. If the effectiveness of the high group in this study may be attributed to a process of dialogic interaction resulting in the negotiation of a text, it is precisely the absence of such negotiation that seems to account for the failure of the other group.

Journals and Learning Logs

Many teachers of high school students in low-achieving classes find journal keeping an effective form of instruction. This is not to say that journals (or anything else) are 100% effective with everyone; Gutierrez (1994) shows that the potential of journal keeping is subverted regularly in many classrooms where teachers respond in the role of critic. Nonetheless journal keeping tends to work when students write about topics of importance to them. Their teachers then read and respond to the content of the entries; they usually do not mark spelling or punctuation. Teachers do not grade these journals, though students receive credit for doing them. Rather than marking and grading them, teachers typically respond in the margins to the content of the entries; comments like "Very interesting! I've thought that too" or "Have you ever stopped to think . . . ?" are not uncommon. The cumulative effect of journal entries and teacher responses is that of a written dialogue or conversation; indeed journal keeping sometimes is called dialogue-journal communication (Staton, Shuy, Kreeft Peyton, & Reed, 1988). Students and teachers take turns speaking just as conversants do. As in conversation, teachers typically pick up on and comment on the substance of the entries, and in so doing, they sustain the dialogue; uptake and level of evaluation are both high.

Even when journals and logs do not address writing skills directly, many students nonetheless improve their writing as a result of keeping them; this improvement may be attributed to frequency of writing, the use of writing to actually communicate ideas (and not just demonstrate skill and mastery), and, related to this, a low level of risk. Yet does journal keeping really provide good practice for more academic writing such as exposition? How much "transfer" can there be in such tasks? Will students write better simply because they write frequently? These questions about practice and transfer misconceive the benefits of both writing development and journal keeping. For while journal entries may be poor models of academic prose, the regular activity of keeping a journal is valuable for helping students get to know their teacher as a reader who is interested in what they have to say and how they think, that is, as someone who is open to their ideas and responds to them, not just someone who assigns homework and evaluates their performance. After they have written journal entries for a while and come to know this interested, receptive reader, they may be more willing to take the kinds of risks required by higher-order thinking and more formal work.

In more structured journals called *learning logs,* students regularly summarize and express their opinions of their readings; learning logs can be especially useful companions to such works of literature as novels and short stories. My own experience as a high school teacher of English is that journals and logs, although generally effective with most students, are particularly useful with students in low-achieving classes because these students especially benefit from regular interaction with a teacher who makes a special effort to listen to and respond to what they have to say. Both journals and learning logs can elicit authentic writing. Learning logs effectively interrelate reading and writing and sometimes classroom discussion as well. Two useful books for teachers on journals and learning logs are Fulwiler's *The Journal Book* (1987) and Staton and colleagues' *Dialogue Journal Communication* (1988).

Position papers can be instructionally effective for similar reasons, especially if students write on issues of importance to them and receive vigorous feedback on the content of their papers. Although most position papers are expository in nature, they need not be, and they need not be limited to high achievers and proficient writers. Elsewhere (Nystrand, 1974) I reported my experience with a remedial and diverse group of ninth graders in which the class first brainstormed what we considered "the most important problem in America today." The problems they identified turned out to be inflation, corrupt public officials, pollution, crime, and population control. Students worked together in task groups devoted to particular problems, and each group collaboratively prepared scripts for brief skits, transcripts from mock interviews, news stories, and position papers in the form of letters suitable for the op-ed page in the local city newspaper. Each group also composed, typed, and mailed a letter to a public official who could do something about their problem. These activities engaged even the most reluctant students, because of the authenticity of the task as well as the high interrelation of writing, reading, and speaking.

DIALOGISM AND STUDENTS AT RISK

These challenging issues become critical when we turn our attention to those students most at risk. These are the students, increasingly representing all demographic and economic strata of American society, whose low literacy skills are topics of continual scrutiny in critiques of American education. The most common strategy for remediation of these students involves first "diagnosing" their weaknesses and then assigning special drills and worksheets to strengthen the targeted weak skills. As we saw in Chapter 2, high school students in low-achieving classes are far more likely than their higher-achieving counterparts to be involved in such contrived, fragmented learning. In language arts and English, this approach almost always makes things worse. This is because such targeting of skills tends to impede learning by weakening its relationship to anything the student already knows. For example, in reading instruction, when students are required to master long lists of specific phonetic combinations and vowel clusters before becoming acquainted with real texts, they usually do so in contrived, dull examples unrelated to anything they can recognize or value. The ineffectiveness of such an approach became clear in Chicago in 1985, for example, when, after having invested 5 years and $8 million in developing a mastery learning reading program, the school board abandoned the effort because students involved in the program were so busy mastering reading objectives that they had no time for actual reading (Shipp, 1985). Students are far more likely to learn to read by grappling with texts that engage their interest and at the same time develop their skills.

Similarly, in writing, when students must contend with long sequences of grammar exercises before moving on to actual writing, or when they must first master all manner of sentence structures before they are allowed to write actual texts or try to communicate anything, the result is all too frequently little more than boredom, reinforced low self-esteem (for being assigned such grunt work), and the utter inability to understand reading and writing as useful and worthwhile processes.

English teachers of low-ability students, our study found, commonly simulate the curriculum of higher-ability classes in a highly superficial way by assigning five-paragraph themes, sentence exercises, and various other sorts of pseudo-discourse, all in the name of "writing" instruction; by teaching abbreviated, fragmented versions of standard titles read in high-ability classes; and by "covering" these titles by asking students to memorize abstracted lists of "facts" from them, all in the name of "literature" instruction. The reason such approaches are ineffective and unengaging is that they violate the terms of reciprocity, and as a result the students are unable to respond except on a superficial, procedural level. These pseudo-forms "filter out" or neutralize the potential benefits of the writing and reading that these students *do* engage in, giving students less experience with writing and discourse than one might conclude from a cursory inspection of the curriculum. This discourse deprivation, not surprisingly, yields poor achievement.

We reported in Chapter 2 that whereas teachers who continuously interrelated writing, reading, and talk significantly improved the ability of students to remember the important details of the literature they had studied, it was authenticity that enabled students to understand and remember the same literature *in depth,* that is, the ability not only to remember details but also to relate and discuss them and interpret their meaning. This was true for students in both high- and low-achieving classes. Given the fact that for students in low-achieving classes, instruction is even less coherent and authentic on average than that of their high-achieving peers, it seems especially important for future researchers to consider how instruction for this latter group of students can be improved.

LITERATURE INSTRUCTION

The nature of literature makes it particularly suitable for dialogic instruction. A literary text is fundamentally different from a news report, involving more than information of the sort that is covered adequately through recitation and short-answer study questions concerning who, what, when, where, and why. Because of this, literature instruction must do more than teach basic textual information; students must learn how to read and respond to the idiosyncratic features of literary texts (Purves, 1991). Skilled readers read such nonfiction texts as newspaper and magazine articles for the main point, making sense of the details only as they seem to relate to it (van Dijk & Kintsch, 1983). By contrast, they read novels and short stories aesthetically by "living through" the narrative with their own experience in mind, savoring "the qualities of the structure, ideas, situations, scenes, personalities, emotions, called forth, participating in the tensions, conflicts, and resolutions as they unfold"

(Rosenblatt, 1988, p. 5). For these reasons, learning how to read and fully experience literature involves personal response, and it is just this process that ample authentic classroom discourse tends to promote.

Unless teachers have themselves experienced literature selections in this way; unless they value literature and can respond to its idiosyncratic qualities; unless they are prepared to model mature responses to literature and elicit students' own personal responses — there is little chance they will succeed in teaching literature effectively. Literature teachers who merely "cover the main points" trivialize literature instruction into sets of poor reading lessons. Classroom discourse that is confined to recitation misses the character of literature; hence, good talk about literature is stifled when the official mode of response is multiple-choice tests and short-answer questions. Effective literature instruction is enhanced by open-ended questions to which students must respond with extended pieces of written prose. In a study of eighth-grade English instruction, I found that effective teachers of literature regularly assign extended pieces of exposition (Nystrand, 1991c). I also found that the frequent use of short-answer exercises in fact degraded overall recall and depth of understanding. This result is consistent with Applebee's (1984) contention that, because writing tends to promote recall of what it focuses on, such "narrow-banded" activities as short-answer questions tend to hinder total recall — in other words, helping students to see the "trees for the forest" hampers their understanding of the overall shape of the forest. In addition, it seems likely that, because they elicit cryptic, fragmented discourse, short-answer exercises promote superficial involvement with literature; in so doing, they trivialize students' experiences with literature. All in all, students learn literature best in classrooms that encourage substantive and personal student response to literature in both classroom interaction and writing. Writing assignments are most effective, moreover, when teachers read them not as examiners but as trusted adults (Britton, Burgess, Martin, McLeod, & Rosen, 1975) seeking to draw out and develop student interpretations of what they have read.

If teachers are to engage students in such substantive conversations, the literature curriculum they teach must not be overspecified with long lists of facts, points, and obligatory principles to teach. Curriculum guides should not dictate teachers' decisions, and teachers must have wide latitude to address major curricular aims in ways that are best for them and their students. For each class, the teacher must have the freedom to work out the curriculum in accordance with the interests, experiences, and capabilities that individual students bring to class.

Because authentic questions have unpredicatable answers, they pose some risk for teachers who do not have an in-depth understanding and feel for the literature they teach. When teachers ask authentic questions and engage their students in substantive conversations, they must be prepared to move with an unfolding discussion that they will not always be able to anticipate fully before class begins and that often cannot be repeated from class to class; for any given class, they will not always be able to anticipate all aspects of the text they may need to discuss. They also must be prepared to deal with the personal responses of their students. The more fully students respond to the text, the more comprehensive, in-depth, and alive the discussion will be. In this sort of discussion, therefore, teachers must have a supple and thorough understanding of the text and be prepared to think quickly on their feet.

High school teachers of students in both low- and high-acheiving classes frequently find Shakespeare's plays difficult to teach. This is due in large measure to the difficulties of Elizabethan verse. Yet the plots are vital and gripping enough to interest most students who can understand them. Some teachers have much greater success with Shakespeare than others, even when they are teaching students in low-achieving classes. Teachers who experience the most difficulties are those who begin by teaching the details of the Globe Theatre as a kind of introduction to Shakespeare, then plod through the plays line by line in close readings of the text, and only at the end show students a movie of the play or take them to a live performance as a kind of climax to the unit. Students in low-achieving classes are not the only ones who fall by the wayside in such an approach that begins with the "parts" of Shakespeare and builds incrementally to the "whole." A far more successful approach reverses this process, starting with the dramatization itself and thus helping students to understand difficult language by hearing and seeing it performed expressively and coherently in context. Rather than building parts to make a whole, this holistic approach makes the parts clear by putting them in context.

As we saw in Chapter 2, many teachers of low-achieving classes feel severely limited when they teach literature. The students in such classes frequently have poor reading skills, and many fail to do homework. As a result, their teachers simply may not assign homework. Instead they may teach literature by reading aloud extremely short texts that leave enough time in class for follow-up questions, seatwork, and occasionally small-group work. If students each take a turn reading aloud a sentence or two to the class — and our study found this to be a fairly common practice — this further fragments the story, especially when the students read haltingly and unexpressively. Consequently, the students fail to become involved over time. It is not surprising that students in such classes fail to remember much about the literature they encounter (one hesitates to say "study"). Unsurprisingly, the experience of students in low-achieving classes with reading and literature, like their experience with writing, is often fragmented, superficial, and unengaging.

As often as possible, literature selections should be full-length novels and dramas — for low- as well as high-ability students. Indeed, the more difficulty students have with the language, the more important it is to engage them in a full, unfragmented story. This is true whether teachers help students with reading problems, writing skills, or literature instruction. If such an approach is important generally, it is positively critical for students in low-achieving classes. There is not room here, of course, to catalogue all of the many ways teachers have found for working effectively with students in low-achieving classes. Much of this work involves teachers first in overcoming long histories of low expectations that these students bring to their classes about both themselves and school. Successful teachers follow their students' voices "into neighborhood corners and alley ways, off the beaten path of the curricular road, where the social action is," as Dyson (1993, p. 7) so eloquently puts it — listening carefully and opening dialogue. Phrasing instruction according to students' abilities, interests, and experience, they take their students seriously, finding — sometimes creating — ways to let their students know that what they think counts.

Appendices

Sample Literature Familiarity Test

1. For each of the following stories that you have read this year, indicate, by checking the correct box, whether each had a happy ending or a sad ending.

   a. "The Adventure of the Speckled Bird"
   b. "The Fifty-first Dragon"
   c. "The Most Dangerous Game"
   d. *Of Mice and Men*

2. Name as many characters as you can remember for each story. If you can't remember their names, briefly describe as many as you can.

3. For as many stories as you can remember, briefly explain how each story ended. Write no more than two sentences for each story.

4. For each story that had a *conflict* you can remember, briefly explain what this conflict was.

   Briefly relate the conflict in *Of Mice and Men* to the ending of the story.

   Briefly relate this conflict in *Of Mice and Men* to the theme of the story.

5. For each story that had a *theme*, or main idea, that you can remember, briefly explain what this theme was.

   Briefly give three reasons why you think the theme of *Of Mice and Men* is what you say.

Scoring Information for Literature Familiarity Test

Categories A–H describe dimensions of interpretive ability. Information from the complete test should be used to derive a score for each.

INFORMATION

A. Extent of recall (absolute scale)

0   None — no detail recognizable from any stories
1   Vague — very few details recognizable for only one or two stories
2   Some details regarding some or most of the stories
3   Many details regarding more than half the stories; richly detailed for less than half the stories
4   Richly detailed — many details regarding more than half of all the stories

B. Depth of understanding (absolute scale)

0   Never goes beyond literal understanding; empty generalization
1   Goes beyond literal understanding for only one story
2   Some evaluation and interpretation of more than one story
3   Some interrelation of story elements in more than one story
4   High interrelation of story elements in most or all stories

C. Number of endings from *stories studied in class* remembered (absolute scale)

0   None
1   One story
2   Two stories
3   Three stories
4   Four stories
5   Five stories

LITERARY UNDERSTANDING

D. Relates ending to denouement

FOR STUDENTS ANSWERING FOR ALL STORIES

1   For either no stories or one (barely)
2   For either one really well or two
3   For three stories
4   For four or five stories

FOR STUDENTS ANSWERING FOR HALF OR LESS OF THE STORIES

1   Almost never or not at all
2   Most of the time
3   Consistently

E. Relates conflict and/or ending to theme

FOR STUDENTS ANSWERING FOR ALL STORIES

1   For either no stories or one (barely)
2   For either one really well or two
3   For three stories
4   For four or five stories

FOR STUDENTS ANSWERING FOR HALF OR LESS OF THE STORIES

1   For either no stories or one (barely)
2   Most of the time
3   Consistently

F. Intuits internal motivations of characters

FOR STUDENTS ANSWERING FOR ALL STORIES

0   For no stories
1   For only one story
2   For less than half the stories
3   For more than half the stories
4   Four out of five or all

FOR STUDENTS ANSWERING FOR HALF OR LESS OF THE STORIES

0   For no stories
1   For less than half the stories
2   For more than half the stories
3   Consistently

G. Interpretive treatment of major selection

0   No response
1   Literal/superficial
2   Literal/substantial
3   Some interpretation
4   Sophisticated and original/substantial

H. Level of discourse regarding theme and conflict

0   No response
1   Cliche or truism
2   Literal
3   General
4   Universal

Note: Score level of discourse the high point reached; that is, if one story is treated literally and two are treated in terms of cliche, record a score of 2 (for literal). Level of discourse should be scored as general if the student goes "beyond the information given" to treat characters, plots, conflicts, etc., in general terms, i.e., offers more than a literal rendition of events, but nonetheless limits these generalizations to the story itself (e.g., statements about what characters are generally like in the story). By contrast, level of discourse should be scored as universal if the student seeks to apply such generalizations beyond the story to experience in general and does so in well developed terms, making an explicit case for the universality of the generalization.

Notes

CHAPTER 1

1. How little things change: In a study of 20 randomly selected English classrooms, Colvin (1931) found that 25% required yes/no answers. For a review of research on recitation, see Duffy (1981); Durkin (1978–79); Hoetker & Ahlbrand (1969); and Sarason (1983).

2. Wells (1993) argues that the function performed by any stretch of discourse is set primarily by the goal of the particular task and relates only indirectly to its genre.

3. A review of literature on dialogism can be found in Nystrand, Greene, & Wiemelt (1993).

4. Vološinov (1973) writes: "The immediate social situation and the broader social milieu wholly determine — and determine from within, so to speak — the structure of an utterance" (p. 86) and, "The organizing center of any utterance, of any experience, is not within but outside — in the social milieu surrounding the individual being" (p. 93).

5. Generally, social constructionism examines the way that shared meanings shape the beliefs, activities, and discourse of members of particular groups, including "interpretive communities" in literature (Fish, 1980) and "discourse communities" in composition (Faigley, 1985). According to these views, the respective communities are said to inform their speakers' discourse, which in turn "reflects" and "instantiates" the group's ideology. These accounts of discourse echo Kuhn's (1970) account of "normal science" whereby scientists' behavior is said to reflect the adopted "paradigms" of their scientific communities, that is, established social conventions and norms. Social constructionist perspectives in literacy include work by Bartholomae (1985) and Shaughnessy (1977) on basic writing (remedial college writing instruction). Other sources include Bizzell (1982), Brodkey (1988), Bruffee (1984, 1986), Rafoth and Rubin (1989), and Rorty (1979).

Social interactionism examines the role played by difference, conflict, and struggle ("stratification, diversity and randomness" [Bakhtin, 1981, p. 272]) in shaping the meaning and discourse of individuals in their interactions with each other. Relevant studies include Brandt (1990), Dyson (1993), Nystrand (1986), Rommetveit (1974, 1992), and Tierney (1983).

For more extensive contrasts of social construction and social interaction, see Nystrand (1990b, 1992; Nystrand, Greene, & Wiemelt, 1993).

6. Bakhtin/Medvedev (1985) writes, "[The concrete utterance] organizes communication oriented toward reciprocal action, and itself reacts" (p. 120).

7. Bakhtin and Vološinov argue that consciousness is constituted by a persistent

struggle and tension between self and other — "the differential relation between a center and all that is not that center" (Holquist, 1990, p. 18) — which in their view is why conflict is essential to the meaning we give our experience and the understandings we have of it. "Consciousness takes shape and being," Vološinov (1973) claims, "in the material of signs created by an organized group in the process of its social interaction" (p. 13).

8. The interactive character of discourse is evident even when the conversants fail to interact: in the conversational management of misunderstandings. When conversants misunderstand one another, they must backtrack to some point in the discourse where they were in synch with each other and properly repair the trouble source; for example, the listener asks, "What?" The ease with which speakers usually explain the "what" — readily, without first asking what was unclear ("What do you mean by 'what?'") — means that speakers consistently monitor their utterances in terms of what their listeners already know.

9. Clark and Holquist (1984) persuasively argue that he also meant the Communist Party.

10. As Klancher (1989) explains, "Bakhtin's crucial starting point — the diversity of practical languages rather than a unitary abstract structure — leads him to argue that every effort to impose unity on these languages is 'monologic.' The institutions of the school, the state, and the church enforce monologic languages as the voice of culture, the voice of authority, the voice of God ventriloquized through the literary critic, the politician, or the priest. His terms *dialogic* and *monologic* thus describe uses of language rather than inherent properties of language itself" (p. 85).

11. James Britton (1969, 1970) argued that conversants are most likely to discover insights when their talk is expressive.

12. "Stratification, diversity, and randomness [i.e., heteroglossia] is (*sic*) not only a static invariant in the life of language, but also what insures its dynamics" (Bakhtin, 1981, p. 272).

13. This formulation follows Halliday's (e.g., 1978) conception of register as a unique configuration of tenor (relationship between conversants), field (what discourse is about), and mode (channel [i.e., written or spoken] and genre).

14. "The understanding of any sign [i.e., learning], whether inner or outer, occurs inextricably tied in with the *situation in which the sign is implemented*. . . . It is always a *social situation*" (Vološinov, 1973, p. 37; emphasis in original).

15. In an analysis of 36 hours of instruction in six different classes, Corey (1940) found that the average student utterance was 11 words long (cited in Hoetker & Ahlbrand, 1969, p. 159).

16. Popper (1972) called this World-3 knowledge, distinguishing it from World-1 knowledge of the physical world and World-2 knowledge of experience and thought.

CHAPTER 2

The section "Small Groups" is reprinted with editorial changes from "Using Small Groups for Response to and Thinking about Literature," by Martin Nystrand,

1. For various reasons, 5 eighth-grade classes were observed only three times.

2. If teachers asked a question that elicited no answer, we coded this as an aborted question, distinguishing it from a repaired question, which is a question that the teacher asks and, without giving students a chance to answer, revises.

We did not code questions unrelated to instruction, rhetorical questions, procedural questions like, "Does that answer your question?" and "Do you have any questions?" or discourse-management questions, which either (a) control discourse traffic (e.g., "What?" or "Did we talk about that?" or "Where are we [in the text]?") or (b) initiate discourse topics (e.g., "Do you remember our discussion from yesterday?").

3. All codings were double checked and challenged by at least one other person besides the coder; we consulted tapes whenever we had questions, and a project assistant verified all transcribed questions and challenged codings by listening to these tapes. A small sample of 12 observations involving over 600 questions was observed by two observers to determine coding reliability: Reliability was computed both at the question level (percent agreement for all questions pooled) and at the observation level (average correlation between raters for the 12 observations).

In our subsample of 12 observations, raters agreed perfectly on authenticity for 78% of 619 questions; the Pearson correlation at the observational level was .938. Raters agreed on uptake perfectly for 81.7% of the 619-question subsample used to check for reliability; at the observational level, the interrater correlation was .973. Raters agreed on cognitive level perfectly for 79.0% of the 619-question subsample used to check for reliability; at the observational level, interrater correlation was .965.

4. CLASS 2.0 and CLASS-EDIT 2.0 and the accompanying documentation are available from the author to anyone wishing to use them. The documentation also contains all coding rules. Write Martin Nystrand, University of Wisconsin–Madison, Wisconsin Center for Education Research, 1025 West Johnson Street, Madison, WI 53706; email NYSTRAND@SSC.WISC.EDU.

5. Students were counted off task in terms of the teacher's expectations. In some classes, teachers expected every student to pay attention during a filmstrip whereas in other classes students were permitted to either watch the filmstrip or do homework; students doing homework were counted as off task in the first class but not in the second.

6. Linguists call such references *deictic* references.

7. To qualify as uptake, a question must incorporate a previous answer, not a previous question; hence, we did not code as uptake teachers' references to questions or remarks they previously had made or to filmstrips, videos, or texts that previously had been discussed. Nor did we code repeated questions as uptake.

8. If a teacher asked students about the previous night's reading, we coded the source of information as text, whereas if the teacher asked about something learned prior to that, even from a text, we coded the source of information as prior knowledge. We made no distinction between prior knowledge and personal knowledge.

9. Superficially a question such as, "Do you think that's important?" might

seem to elicit a record (i.e., referring to what the student is thinking at the time of the question), but the question more typically elicits a higher-cognitive operation such as an analysis of what is important. Hence, for such preformulated questions (cf. French & Maclure, 1981), we distinguished the preformulators ("Do you think . . .") from their nuclear utterances (the remainder of the question: "Is that important?"), coding only the latter.

10. More than half of the eighth-grade classes (58.6%) spent no time at all in discussion; 20.7% spent 1 minute or more on average; only two classes of the 58 regularly spent 7 minutes or more. In ninth grade, 61.1% of all classes had no discussion at all, and only 5.6% had more than a minute daily; only one class of the 54 averaged more than 2 minutes.

11. In grade 8, 91.4% of all classes spent no time in small-group work; only 5 out of 58 classes involved small-group work, and this ranged from an average of 1.75–13.50 minutes. In grade 9, 63% of all classes had no small-group work at all; only 11.1% spent more than 5 minutes daily; and only four classes spent more than 10 minutes daily in small groups.

12. In 36.2% of the eighth-grade classes, teachers asked 5% or fewer authentic questions. Only 6.9% of classes involved more than 30% authentic teacher questions; one class of the 58 involved more than 50%. In 25.9% of the classes, uptake was present 5% or less. Only 8.6% of classes involved more than 20%; two classes involved 28%.

13. In grade 9, 13% of all classes had 50% or more; and in one class, the teacher on average asked 83% authentic questions. Uptake was noted in all ninth-grade classes, although 5.6% of classes involved less than 10%. Half the classes had at least 25%, and 13% of classes involved 40% or more uptake.

14. Four of these titles were chosen as a stratified sample to represent the kinds of literature each class had studied; if half of the titles studied were short stories, then two of the four were short stories, and so on. The fifth selected title was the one work the class had spent the most time on; typically it was either a novel, such as *To Kill a Mockingbird* or *A Tale of Two Cities,* or a drama, such as *Romeo and Juliet.*

15. Information on student characteristics came from student questionnaires. Race and ethnicity were coded when students identified themselves as Black or Hispanic. Family socioeconomic status was indicated by an unweighted additive composite of father's and mother's education, the higher of either parent's occupational status, and a list of home resources, as reported on student questionnaires. Fall reading skills were measured by a NAEP multiple-choice test of reading comprehension, and fall writing skills were measured by a holistically scored writing sample. Fall writing skills were indicated by a writing sample that was scored by two readers, whose marks were averaged, for (a) level of abstraction, based on Britton and colleagues' (1975) categories of transactional-informative prose; and (b) coherence and elaborateness of argumentation, based on the 1979/1984 NAEP criteria for informative writing (in Applebee, Langer, & Mullis, 1985). Each student's writing score was the sum of these two measures. Interrater reliability of scoring this test was .68. (For further details on the background variables and achievement controls, see Gamoran & Nystrand, 1991).

16. The relationship between student autonomy and knowledge production has

been found in many studies, including studies examining small groups; see King (1992) and Palincsar, David, Winn, Stevens, and Brown (1990).

17. Some small-group work rated lowest on autonomy and student production of knowledge concerned grammar and sentence errors, not literature. All of the highest-rated small-group work concerned literature. We are unable to rule out, for the lowest-rated, small-group sessions, the possibility that their focus on grammar and sentence correction rather than literature, accounted for the negative impact of collaborative seatwork on literature achievement.

CHAPTER 3

We wish to acknowledge Sarah Bing-Prineas's invaluable help in the early stages of this research.

1. These predictions were the result of a residual analysis based on instructional and background variables outlined in Chapter 2.

2. Students in classes whose format most closely approximated conversation tended to score higher on the literature achievement test, regardless of the actual number of student or teacher questions.

CHAPTER 4

Parts of the sections "Dialogism and Students at Risk" (pp. 104–105) and "Literature Instruction" (pp. 105–108) are reprinted with editorial changes from "High School English Students in Low-Ability Classes: What Helps?" by Martin Nystrand, *The Newsletter of the National Center on Effective Secondary Schools,* January 1990, pp. 7–8.

1. "The meaning of a word is determined entirely by its context. In fact, there are as many meanings of a word as there are contexts of its usage" (Vološinov, 1973 p. 79). Compare also Vološinov's (1973) observation that *"the forms of signs are conditioned above all by the social organization of the participants involved and also by the immediate conditions of their interaction.* When these forms change, so does sign" (p. 21; emphasis in translation).

2. Vološinov (1973) argues that thought, or inner speech, "resemble[s] the *alternating lines of a dialogue* . . . joined with one another and alternat[ing] with one another not according to the laws of grammar or logic but according to the laws of *evaluative* (emotive) *correspondence, dialogical deployment*, etc., in close dependence on the historical conditions of the social situation and the whole pragmatic run of life" (p. 38; emphasis in translation).

3. When writers fail to elaborate potential trouble sources or do so inadequately, the result is "misconstraint," that is, a mismatch between what the writer has to say and what the reader needs to find out. If the topic is inadequately elaborated, the reader will find the text *abstruse* (What's this about?). If the writer inadequately elaborates what is said about the topic, the reader will find the text *ambiguous* (So what's the point?). For more, see Nystrand (1986, Ch. 3).

References

Applebee, A. N. (1981). *Writing in the secondary school* (Research Rep. No. 21). Urbana, IL: National Council of Teachers of English.

Applebee, A. N. (1982). Writing and learning in school settings. In M. Nystrand (Ed.), *What writers know: The language, process, and structure of written discourse* (pp. 365–381). New York & London: Academic Press.

Applebee, A. N. (1984). Writing and reasoning. *Review of Educational Research, 54,* 577–596.

Applebee, A. N., Langer, J. A., & Mullis, I. V. S. (1985). *Writing: Trends across the decade, 1974–84* (Report No. 15-W-01). Princeton, NJ: Educational Testing Service.

Applebee, A., Langer, J., Mullis, I., Latham., A., & Gentile, C. (1994). *NAEP 1992 writing report card*. Washington, DC: U.S. Government Printing Office for National Center for Education Statistics.

Bakhtin, M. (1981). *The dialogic imagination*. Austin: University of Texas Press.

Bakhtin, M. (1984). *Problems of Dostoevsky's poetics* (C. Emerson, Trans.). Minneapolis: University of Minnesota Press.

Bakhtin, M./Medvedev, P. N. (1985). *The formal method in literary scholarship: A critical introduction to sociological poetics*. Cambridge, MA: Harvard University Press.

Bakhtin, M. (1986). *Speech genres & other late essays* (V. W. McGee, Trans; C. Emerson & M. Holquist, Eds.). Austin: University of Texas.

Barnes, D. (1976). *Communication and the curriculum*. London: Penguin.

Barnes, D., & Schemilt, D. (1974). Transmission and interpretation. *Educational Review, 26,* 213–228.

Bartholomae, D. (1985). Inventing the university. In M. Rose (Ed.), *When a writer can't write* (pp. 134–165). New York: Guilford Press.

Becker, A. L. (1992a). A short essay on languaging. In F. Steier (Ed.), *Research and reflexivity* (pp. 226–234). Newbury Park, CA: Sage.

Becker, A. L. (1992b). Silence across languages: An essay. In C. Kramsch & S. McConnell-Ginet (Eds.), *Text and context: Cross-disciplinary perspectives* (pp. 115–123). Lexington, MA: Heath.

Bellack, A., Kliebard, H., Hyman, R., & Smith, F. (1966). *The language of the classroom*. New York: Teachers College Press.

Benson, N. (1979). *The effects of peer feedback during the writing process on writing performance, revision behavior, and attitude toward writing*. Unpublished Ph.D. dissertation, University of Colorado, Boulder.

Berkenkotter, C. (1981). Understanding a writer's awareness of audience. *College Composition and Communication, 32,* 388–399.

Bickard, M. H. (1987). The social nature of the functional nature of language. In M.

Hickmann (Ed.), *Social and functional approaches to language and thought.* Orlando: Academic Press.

Bissex, G. (1980). *Gnys at wrk: A child learns to write and read.* Cambridge, MA: Harvard University Press.

Bizzell, P. (1982). Cognition, convention, and certainty: What we need to know about writing. *Pre/Text, 3,* 213–243.

Bloome, D., & Argumedo, B. (1983). Procedural display and classroom interaction: Another look at academic engaged time. In T. Erg (Ed.), *Middle school research: Selected studies* (pp. 1–20). Columbus, OH: National Middle School Association.

Bloome, D., Puro, P., & Theodorou, E. (1989). Procedural display and classroom lessons. *Curriculum Inquiry, 19,* 265–291.

Brandt, D. (1990). *Literacy as involvement: The acts of writers, readers, and texts.* Carbondale: Southern Illinois University Press.

Britton, J. (1969). Talking to learn. In D. Barnes, J. Britton, & H. Rosen (Eds.), *Language, the learner, and the school* (pp. 79–115). Harmondsworth: Penguin.

Britton, J. (1970). *Language and learning.* London: Allen Lane-Penguin.

Britton, J., Burgess, T., Martin, N., McLeod, A., & Rosen, H. (1975). *The development of writing abilities: 11–18.* London: Macmillan.

Brodkey, L. (1988). *Academic writing as social practice.* Philadelphia: Temple University Press.

Bruffee, K. (1984). Collaborative learning and the 'conversation of mankind.' *College English, 46,* 635–652.

Bruffee, K. (1986). Social construction, language, and the authority of knowledge. *College English, 48,* 773–790.

Bruner, J. S. (1966). *Toward a theory of instruction.* Cambridge, MA: Harvard University Press, Belknap Press.

Bruner, J. (1978). The role of dialogue in language acquisition. In A. Sinclair et al. (Eds.), *The child's conception of language* (pp. 241–256). New York: Springer-Verlag.

Bruner, J. S. (1981). The social context of language acquisition. *Language and Communication, 1,* 155–178.

Burgess, T. A. (1985). Curriculum process and the role of writing. In M. Chorny (Ed.), *Teacher as learner: Language in the classroom project.* Alberta: University of Calgary.

Burstall, S. (1909). *Impressions of American education in 1908.* London: Longmans, Green.

Carlsen, W. S. (1991). Questioning in classrooms: A sociolinguistic perspective. *Review of Educational Research, 61,* 157–178.

Cazden, C. (1988). *Classroom discourse: The language of teaching and learning.* Portsmouth, NH: Heinemann.

Cazden, C. (in press). Selective traditions: Readings of Vygotsky in writing pedagogy. In D. Hicks (Ed.), *Child discourse and social learning: An interdisciplinary perspective.* New York: Cambridge University Press.

Clark, K., & Holquist, M. (1984). *Mikhail Bakhtin.* Cambridge, MA: Belknap Press of Harvard University Press.

Cohen, E. (1986). *Designing groupwork: Strategies for the heterogeneous classroom.* New York: Teachers College Press.

Cohen, M., & Riel, M. (1989). The effect of distant audiences on students' writing. *American Educational Research Journal, 26,* 143–159.

Collins, J. (1982). Discourse style, classroom interaction and differential treatment. *Journal of Reading Behavior, 14,* 429–437.

Colvin, S. (1919). The most common faults of beginning high school teachers. In G. M. Whipple & H. L. Miller (Eds.), *The professional preparation of high school teachers* (Eighteenth Yearbook of the National Society for the Study of Education, Part I, pp. 262–272). Bloomington, IL: Public School Publishing.

Colvin, S. (1931). *An introduction to high school teaching.* New York: Macmillan.

Corey, S. (1940). Some implications of verbatim records of high school classroom talk. NEA Proceedings, pp. 371–372.

Daiute, C. (1986). Do 1 and 2 make 2? Patterns of influence by young coauthors. *Written Communication, 3,* 382–408.

Daiute, C. (1989). Play as thought: Thinking strategies of young writers. *Harvard Educational Review, 59,* 1–23.

Daiute, C., & Dalton, B. (1989). 'Let's brighten it up a bit': Collaboration and cognition in writing. In B. Rafoth & D. Rubin (Eds.), *The social construction of written communication.* Norwood, NJ: ABLEX.

Daiute, C., & Dalton, B. (1993). Collaboration between children learning to write: Can novices be masters? *Cognition and Instruction, 10,* 1–43.

Daiute, C., & Griffin, T. M. (1993). The social construction of narrative. In C. Daiute (Ed.), *The development of literacy through social interaction* (pp. 97–120). San Francisco, CA: Jossey-Bass.

Dale, H. (1992). *Collaborative writing: A singular we.* Unpublished doctoral dissertation, University of Wisconsin-Madison.

DiPardo, A., & Freedman, S. (1988). Peer response groups in the writing classroom: Theoretic foundations and new directions. *Review of Educational Research, 58,* 119–149.

Drew, P., & Heritage, J. (1992). *Talk at work: Interaction in institutional settings.* Cambridge: Cambridge University Press.

Duffy, G. (1981). Teacher effectiveness research: Implications for the reading profession. In M. Kamil (Ed.), *Directions in reading: Research and instruction* (Thirtieth Yearbook of the National Reading Conference, pp. 113–136). Washington, DC: National Reading Conference.

Durkin, D. (1978–79). What classroom observations reveal about reading comprehension instruction. *Reading Research Quarterly, 14,* 481–533.

Dyson, A. (1989). *Multiple worlds of child writers: Friends learning to write.* New York: Teachers College Press.

Dyson, A. (1993). *The social worlds of children learning to write in an urban primary school.* New York: Teachers College Press.

Eder, D. (1982). Differences in communicative styles across ability groups. In L. C. Wilkinson (Ed.), *Communicating in the classroom* (pp. 245–264). New York: Academic Press.

Fagan, E. R., Hassler, D. M., & Szabl, M. (1981). Evaluation of questioning strategies in language arts instruction. *Research in the Teaching of English, 15,* 267–273.

Faigley, L. (1985). Nonacademic writing: The social perspective. In L. Odell &

D. Goswami (Eds.), *Writing in nonacademic settings* (pp. 231–248). New York: Guilford.

Farr, M., & Elías-Olivares, L. (1988). *Mexican American language and literacy in Chicago: A study of two neighborhoods.* Proposal to the National Science Foundation, Linguistics Program.

Fish, S. (1980). *Is there a text in this class? The authority of interpretive communities.* Cambridge, MA: Harvard University Press.

Flanders, N. A. (1970). *Analyzing teaching behavior.* Reading, MA: Addison-Wesley.

Flower, L., & Hayes, J. R. (1977). Problem-solving strategies and the writing process. *College English, 39,* 449–461.

Forman, E. A., & Cazden, C. B. (1985). Exploring Vygotskian perspectives in education: The cognitive value of peer interaction. In J. Wertsch (Ed.), *Culture, communication, and cognition: Vygotskian perspectives.* Cambridge: Cambridge University Press.

Fox, R. (1980). Treatment of writing apprehension and its effects on composition. *Research in the Teaching of English, 14,* 39–49.

French, P., & Maclure, M. (1981). Teachers' questions, pupils' answers: An investigation of questions and answers in the infant classroom. *First Language, 2,* 31–45.

Freire, P. (1970). *Pedagogy of the oppressed.* New York: Seabury.

Fulwiler, T. (Ed.). (1987). *The journal book.* Portsmouth, NH: Boynton-Cook.

Gamoran, A., & Berends, M. (1987). The effects of stratification in secondary schools: Synthesis of survey and ethnographic research. *Review of Educational Research, 57,* 415–435.

Gamoran, A., & Nystrand, M. (1991). Background and instructional effects on achievement in eighth-grade English and social studies. *Journal of Research on Adolescence, 1,* 277–300.

Gamoran, A., & Nystrand, M. (1992). Taking students seriously. In F. Newmann (Ed.), *Student engagement and achievement in American secondary schools* (pp. 40–61). New York: Teachers College Press.

Gamoran, A., Nystrand, M., Berends, M., & LePore, P. C. (1995). An organizational analysis of the effects of ability grouping. *American Educational Research Journal, 32,* 687–715.

Gere, A., & Stevens, R. (1985). The language of writing groups: How oral response shapes revision. In S. Freedman (Ed.), *The acquisition of written language: Revision and response* (pp. 85–105). Norwood, NJ: ABLEX.

Goodlad, J. I. (1984). *A place called school: Prospects for the future.* New York: McGraw-Hill.

Goodwin, C. (1981). *Conversational organization: Interaction between speakers and hearers.* New York: Academic Press.

Gundlach, R. (1982). Children as writers. In M. Nystrand (Ed.), *What writers know: The language, process, and structure of written discourse* (pp. 129–147). New York and London: Academic Press.

Gutierrez, K. (1991, April). *The effects of writing process instruction on Latino children.* Paper presented at the annual meeting of the American Educational Research Association, Chicago.

Gutierrez, K. (1992, April). *The social contexts of literacy instruction for Latino children.*

Paper presented at the annual meeting of the American Educational Research Association, San Francisco.

Gutierrez, K. (1993, April). *Scripts, counterscripts, and multiple scripts.* Paper presented at the annual meeting of the American Educational Research Association, Atlanta.

Gutierrez, K. (1994). How talk, context, and script shape contexts for learning: A cross-comparison of journal writing. *Linguistics and Education, 5,* 335–365.

Halliday, M. A. K. (1978). *Language as social semiotic: The social interpretation of language and meaning.* Baltimore: University Park Press.

Heath, S. B. (1978). Teacher talk: Language in the classroom. *Language in Education: Theory and Practice, 1,* 1–30.

Heath, S. B. (1980, November). *What no bedtime story means: Narrative skills at home and school.* Paper prepared for the Terman Conference, Stanford University, Stanford, CA.

Heath, S. B. (1983). *Ways with words: Language, life, and work in communities and classrooms.* New York: Cambridge University Press.

Heath, S. B., & Branscombe, A. (1985). "Intelligent writing" in an audience community: Teacher, students, and researcher. In S. Freedman (Ed.), *The acquisition of written language: Revision and response* (pp. 3–32). Norwood, NJ: ABLEX.

Hillocks, G., Jr. (1986). *Research on written communication: New directions for teaching.* Urbana, IL: National Conference on Research in English.

Hirsch, E., Jr. (1987). *Cultural literacy: What every American needs to know.* Boston: Houghton Mifflin.

Hoetker, J. (1967). Analyses of the subject matter related verbal behavior in nine junior high school English classes. Unpublished Ed.D. dissertation, Washington University, St. Louis.

Hoetker, J., & Ahlbrand, W. P., Jr. (1969). The persistence of the recitation. *American Education Research Journal, 6,* 145–167.

Holquist, M. (1983). The politics of representation. *The Quarterly Newsletter of the Laboratory of Comparative Human Cognition, 5,* 2–9.

Holquist, M. (1990). *Dialogism: Bakhtin and his world.* London: Routledge.

Honea, M. (1982). Wait time as an instructional variable: An influence on teacher and student. *Clearinghouse, 56,* 167–170.

Huston, B., & Thompson, D. (1985). Moving language around on the word processor: Cognitive operations upon language. *The Quarterly Newsletter of the Laboratory of Comparative Human Cognition, 7,* 57–64.

Hynds, S. (1991). Questions of difficulty in literary reading. In A. Purves (Ed.), *The idea of difficulty in literature and literature learning: Joining theory and practice* (pp. 117–140). Albany: State University of New York at Albany Press.

King, A. (1992). Facilitating elaborative learning through guided student-generated questioning. *Educational Psychologist, 27,* 111–126.

Klancher, J. (1989). Bakhtin's rhetoric. In P. Donahue & E. Quandahl (Eds.), *Reclaiming pedagogy: The rhetoric of the classroom* (pp. 83–96). Carbondale & Edwardsville: Southern Illinois University Press.

Kuhn, T. S. (1970). *The structure of scientific revolutions* (2nd ed.). Chicago: University of Chicago Press.

Labov, W. (1969). *The logic of nonstandard English* (Georgetown Monographs on Language and Linguistics, Vol. 22). Washington, DC: Georgetown University Press.

Lagana, J. (1973). *The development, implementation, and evaluation of a model for teaching composition which utilizes individualized learning and peer grouping.* Unpublished doctoral dissertation, University of Pittsburgh.

Langer, J. A. (1995). *Envisioning literature: Literary understanding and literature instruction.* New York: Teachers College Press.

Langer, J. A., & Applebee, A. N. (1984). Language, learning, and interaction: A framework for improving instruction. In A. N. Applebee, *Contexts for learning to write: Studies of secondary school instruction* (pp. 169–181). Norwood, NJ: ABLEX.

Langer, J. A., & Applebee, A. N. (1987). *How writing shapes thinking: A study of teaching and learning* (Research Rep. No. 22). Urbana, IL: National Council of Teachers of English.

Lemke, J. (1988). Genres, semantics, and classroom education. *Linguistics and Education, 1,* 81–99.

Leont'ev, A. A. (1981). The problem of activity in psychology. In J. V. Wertsch (Ed.), *The concept of activity in Soviet psychology* (pp. 37–71). Armonk, NY: M. E. Sharpe.

Lotman, Y. M. (1988). Text within a text. *Soviet Psychology, 26,* 32–51.

Martin, N., D'Arcy, P., Newton, B., & Parker, R. (1976). *Writing and learning across the curriculum.* London: Ward Lock Educational.

Mehan, H. (1979a). "What time is it, Denise?": Asking known information questions in classroom discourse. *Theory into Practice, 18,* 285–294.

Mehan, H. (1979b). *Learning lessons.* Cambridge, MA: Harvard University Press.

Michaels, S. (1987). Text and context: A new approach to the study of classroom writing. *Discourse Processes, 10,* 321–346.

Miller, G. (1956). The magic number seven, plus or minus two: Some limits on our capacity for processing information. *Psychological Review, 63,* 81–92.

Miller, W. (1922). The administrative use of intelligence tests in the high school. In G. M. Whipple (Ed.), *The administrative use of intelligence tests* (Twenty-first Yearbook of the National Society for the Study of Education, Part II, pp. 189–222). Bloomington, IL: Public School Publishing.

Moffett, J. (1968). *Teaching the universe of discourse.* Boston: Houghton Mifflin.

Moll, L. (1990). Introduction. In. L. Moll (Ed.), *Vygotsky and education: Instructional implications and applications of sociohistorical psychology* (pp. 1–27). New York: Cambridge University Press.

Newmann, F. M. (1988, January). Can depth replace coverage in the high school curriculum? *Phi Delta Kappan, 69,* 345–348.

Newmann, F. (1990). Higher order thinking in teaching social studies: A rationale for the assessment of classroom thoughtfulness. *Journal of Curriculum Studies, 22,* 41–56.

Nystrand, M. (1974). Lesson plans for the open classroom. *English Journal, 63,* 79–81.

Nystrand, M. (1983). The role of context in written communication. *The Nottingham Linguistic Circular, 12,* 55–65.

Nystrand, M. (1986). *The structure of written communication: Studies in reciprocity between writers and readers.* Orlando & London: Academic Press.

Nystrand, M. (1987). The context of written communication. In R. Horowitz & S. J. Samuels (Eds.), *Comprehending oral and written language* (pp. 197–214). Orlando & London: Academic Press.

Nystrand, M. (1990a). *CLASS 2.0 user's manual*. Madison, WI: National Center on Effective Secondary Schools.

Nystrand, M. (1990b). Sharing words: The effects of readers on developing writers. *Written Communication, 7,* 3–24.

Nystrand, M. (1991a, April). *On the negotiation of understanding between students and teachers: Towards a social-interactionist model of school learning.* Paper presented at the annual meeting of the American Educational Research Association, Chicago.

Nystrand, M. (1991b, May). [Interviewed by A. Lockwood]. Beyond filling in blanks [Special issue]. *Focus in Change,* p. 7.

Nystrand, M. (1991c). Making it hard: Curriculum and instruction as factors in the difficulty of literature. In A. Purves (Ed.), *The idea of difficulty in literature and literature learning: Joining theory and practice* (pp. 141–156). Albany: State University of New York at Albany Press.

Nystrand, M. (1992). Social interactionism versus social constructionism: Bakhtin, Rommetveit, and the semiotics of written text. In A. H. Wold (Ed.), *The dialogical alternative: Towards a theory of language and mind* (pp. 157–173). Oslo: Scandinavian University Press.

Nystrand, M. (1993, November 20). *On the dialogic nature of discourse and learning.* Paper presented at colloquium, The Social Construction of Literacy: Perspectives and Issues for Integration, sponsored by the Research Assembly of the National Council of Teachers of English, Pittsburgh.

Nystrand, M., & Brandt, D. (1989). Response to writing as a context for learning to write. In C. Anson (Ed.), *Writing and response: Theory, practice, and research* (pp. 209–230). Urbana, IL: National Council of Teachers of English.

Nystrand, M., & Gamoran, A. (1988, April). *A study of instruction as discourse.* Paper presented at the annual meeting of the American Educational Research Association, San Francisco.

Nystrand, M., & Gamoran, A. (1991a). Instructional discourse, student engagement, and literature achievement. *Research in the Teaching of English, 25,* 261–290.

Nystrand, M., & Gamoran, A. (1991b). Student engagement: When recitation becomes conversation. In H. Waxman & H. Walberg (Eds.), *Effective teaching: Current research* (pp. 257–276). Berkeley: McCutchan.

Nystrand, M., Gamoran, A., & Heck, M. J. (1992, January). Using small groups for response to and thinking about literature. *English Journal, 83,* 14–22.

Nystrand, M., Greene, S., & Wiemelt, J. (1993, July). Where did composition studies come from? An intellectual history. *Written Communication, 10,* 267–333.

Nystrand, M., & Wiemelt, J. (1991). When is a text explicit? Formalist and dialogical conceptions. *Text, 11,* 25–41.

Olson, D. R. (1977). From utterance to text: The bias of language in speech and writing. *Harvard Educational Review, 47,* 257–281.

Olson, D. (1981). Writing: The divorce of the author from the text. In B. Kroll & R. Vann (Eds.), *Exploring speaking-writing relationships: Connections and contrasts* (pp. 99–110). Urbana, IL: National Council of Teachers of English.

Olson, D. (1991). Children's understanding of interpretation and the autonomy of written texts. *Text, 11,* 3–23.

Page, R. N. (1991). *Lower-track classrooms: A curricular and cultural perspective.* New York: Teachers College Press.

Palincsar, A. S., & Brown, A. L. (1984). Reciprocal teaching of comprehension-fostering and monitoring activities. *Cognition and Instruction, 1,* 117–175.

Palincsar, A. S., David, Y. M., Winn, J., Stevens, D., & Brown, A. L. (1990, April). *Examining the differential effects of teacher- versus student-controlled activity in comprehension instruction.* Paper presented at annual meeting of American Educational Research Association, Boston.

Perret-Clermont, A. N. (1980). *Social interaction and cognitive development in children.* New York: Academic Press.

Piaget, J. (1951). *Play, dreams, and imitation.* London: Routledge & Kegan Paul.

Polanyi, M. (1958). *Personal knowledge.* London: Routledge & Kegan Paul.

Popper, K. (1972). *Objective knowledge: An evolutionary approach.* London: Oxford at the Clarendon Press.

Powell, A., Farrar, E., & Cohen, D. K. (1985). *The shopping-mall high school.* Boston: Houghton Mifflin.

Pressley, M., Wood, E., Woloshyn, V. E., Martin. V., King, A., & Menke, D. (1992). Encouraging mindful use of prior knowledge: Attempting to construct explanatory answers facilitates learning. *Educational Psychologist, 27,* 91–110.

Purves, A. (1991). Indeterminate texts, responsive readers, and the idea of difficulty in literature. In A. Purves (Ed.), *The idea of difficulty in literature and literature learning: Joining theory and practice* (pp. 157–170). Albany: State University of New York at Albany Press.

Rafoth, B., & Rubin, D. (Eds.). (1989). *The social construction of written communication.* Norwood, NJ: ABLEX.

Rommetveit, R. (1974). *On message structure: A framework for the study of language and communication.* London: Wiley.

Rommetveit, R. (1983). In search of a truly interdisciplinary semantics. A sermon on hopes of salvation from hereditary sins. *Journal of Semantics, 2,* 1–28.

Rommetveit, R. (1992). Outlines of a dialogically based social-cognitive approach to human cognition and communication. In A. H. Wold (Ed.), *The dialogical alternative: Towards a theory of language and mind* (19–44). Oslo: Scandinavian University Press.

Rorty, R. (1979). *Philosophy and the mirror of nature.* Princeton, NJ: Princeton University Press.

Rosen, H. (1992). The politics of writing. In K. Kimberley, M. Meek, & J. Miller (Eds.), *New readings: Contributions to an understanding of literacy.* London: A & C Black.

Rosenblatt, L. (1938). *Literature as exploration.* New York: Appleton-Century.

Rosenblatt, L. (1988). *Writing and reading: The transactional theory* (Tech. Rep. No. 13). Berkeley: Center for the Study of Writing.

Sacks, H., Schegloff, E. A., & Jefferson, G. (1974). A simplest systematics for the organization of turn-taking in conversation. *Language, 50,* 696–735.

Sarason, S. (1983). *Schooling in America: Scapegoat and salvation.* New York: Free Press.

Schultz, J., Erickson, F., & Florio, S. (1982). Where's the floor? Aspects of the cultural organization of social relationships in communication at home and in school. In P. Gilmore & A. Glatthorn (Eds.), *Children in and out of school: Ethnography and education* (pp. 88–123). Washington, DC: Center for Applied Linguistics.

Schutz, A. (1967). *Collected papers: Vol. 1. The problem of social reality.* The Hague: Martinus Nijhoff.

Scollon, R., & Scollon, S. B. (1980). *The literate two-year old: The fictionalization of self* [Typescript]. University of Alaska, Center for Cross-Cultural Studies.

Shaughnessy, M. (1977). *Errors and expectations.* New York: Oxford University Press.

Shipp, E. R. (1985, October 8). New theory on reading goes awry. *New York Times,* pp. C1–2.

Sizer, T. (1984). *Horace's compromise.* Boston: Houghton Mifflin.

Smith, F. (1971). *Understanding reading.* New York: Holt, Rinehart, and Winston.

Sperling, M. (1991). Dialogues of deliberation: Conversation in the teacher — student writing conference. *Written Communication, 8,* 131–162.

Stallings, J. A., & Stipek, D. (1986). Research on early childhood and elementary school teaching programs. In M. C. Wittrock (Ed.), *Handbook of research on teaching* (3rd ed.; pp. 727–753). New York: Macmillan.

Staton, J., Shuy, R., Kreeft Peyton, J., & Reed, L. (1988). *Dialogue journal communication: Classroom, linguistic, social and cognitive views.* Norwood, NJ: ABLEX.

Stevens, R. (1912). *The question as a measure of efficiency in instruction: A critical study of classroom practice* (Contributions to Education No. 48). New York: Teachers College, Columbia University.

Sweigart, W. (1991). Classroom talk, knowledge development, and writing. *Research in the Teaching of English, 25,* 497–509.

Teale, W., & Sulzby, E. (Eds.). (1986). *Emergent literacy: Writing and reading.* Norwood, NJ: ABLEX.

Tharp, R., & Gallimore, R. (1988). *Rousing minds to life: Teaching, learning, and schooling in social context.* New York: Cambridge University Press.

Thayer, V. (1928). *The passing of the recitation.* Boston: D. C. Heath.

Tierney, R. (1983). Writer-reader transactions: A synthesis and suggested directions. *Language Arts, 30,* 627–642.

Tierney, R., & LaZansky, J. (1980). *The rights and responsibilities of readers and writers: A contractual agreement* (Education Rep. No. 15). Urbana: University of Illinois, Center for the Study of Reading.

van Dijk, T., & Kintsch, W. (1983). *Strategies of discourse comprehension.* New York: Academic Press.

Vološinov, V. N. (1973). *Marxism and the philosophy of language* (L. Matejka & I. R. Titunik, Trans.). New York: Seminar Press.

Vološinov, V. N. (1976). *Freudianism, a Marxist critique* (I. R. Titunik, Trans.). New York: Academic Press.

Vygotsky, L. (1978). *Mind in society.* Cambridge, MA: Harvard University Press.

Wells, G. (1993). Reevaluating the IRF sequence: A proposal for the articulation of theories of acitivity and discourse for the analysis of teaching and learning in the classroom. *Linguistics and Education, 5,* 1–37.

Wertsch, J. V. (Ed.). (1979). *The concept of activity in Soviet psychology.* New York: Merril Sharpe.

Wertsch, J. V. (1985). The semiotic mediation of mental life: L. S. Vygotsky and M. M. Bakhtin. In E. Mertz & R. Parmentier (Eds.), *Semiotic mediation: Sociocultural and psychological perspectives* (pp. 49–71). Orlando: Academic Press.

Wertsch, J. V. (1991). *Voices of the mind: A sociocultural approach to mediated action.* Cambridge, MA: Harvard University Press.

Wertsch, J. V., & Hickmann, M. (1987). Problem solving in social interaction: A microgenetic analysis. In M. Hickmann (Ed.), *Social and functional approaches to language and thought* (pp. 251–266). New York: Academic Press.

Wertsch, J. V., & Toma, C. (1990, April). *Discourse and learning in the classroom: A sociocultural approach.* Presentation at the University of Georgia Visiting Lecturer Series on Constructivism in Education, Atlanta.

Wittrock, M. (1990). Generative processes of comprehension. *Educational Psychologist, 24,* 345–376.

Wittrock, M. C., & Alesandrini, K. (1990). Generation of summaries and analogies and analytic and holistic abilities. *American Education Research Journal, 27,* 489–502.

Yalom, I. D. (1995). *The theory and practice of group psychotherapy* (4th ed.). New York: Basic Books.

Index

About the Authors

Martin Nystrand is Professor of English at the University of Wisconsin–Madison, Wisconsin director of the National Research Center on English Learning and Achievement and co-editor of *Written Communication*. Since taking his Ph.D. in English education from Northwestern University in 1974, he has been awarded a Spencer Foundation grant, named a fellow of the National Conference on Research in English, served as president of the AERA SIG for Writing Research, and been entered in *Who's Who in American Education*. He is the author of *The Structure of Written Communication: Studies in Reciprocity Between Writers and Readers* (1986) and the editor of *What Writers Know: The Language, Process, and Structure of Written Discourse* (1982) and *Language as a Way of Knowing: A Book of Readings* (1977), along with numerous scholarly articles, contributed chapters, and specialized encyclopedia entries.

Adam Gamoran is Professor of Sociology and Educational Policy Studies at the University of Wisconsin–Madison. A former Fulbright scholar and Spencer Fellow, he took his Ph.D. in the sociology of education from the University of Chicago in 1984 and has published a number of scholarly articles. **Robert M. Kachur** is Assistant Professor of Nineteenth-Century Literature and Composition at the University of Massachusetts–Lowell. He received his Ph.D. in 19th-century British literature in 1996 from the University of Wisconsin–Madison, where he earned numerous awards and fellowships. **Catherine Prendergast** is in the Department of English at the University of Wisconsin–Madison. She graduated cum laude from Columbia University, received a master's degree from the University of Wisconsin–Madison, and has presented papers at several symposia.